FROM LINE TO DESIGN

DESIGN GRAPHICS COMMUNICATION

THIRD EDITION

Scott VanDyke

VAN NOSTRAND REINHOLD
_____ New York

ACKNOWLEDGMENTS

I am grateful for the assistance of many people who helped me complete this project. Among the many, I would like to recognize the following:

My wife Cyd and my boys for tolerating an often non-existent husband and father.

Special thanks to Maas Grassli and Associates, Land Planners, Salt Lake City, Utah, and to Allred, Soffe, Tuttle & Wilkinson, Inc., Murray, Utah.

Library of Congress Catalog Card Number 89-70627

ISBN 0-442-00113-4

I(T)P   Van Nostrand Reinhold is a division of International Thomson Publishing.
ITP logo is a trademark under license.

Printed in the United States of America

Van Nostrand Reinhold
115 Fifth Avenue
New York, New York 10003

International Thomson Publishing
Berkshire House
168-173 High Holborn
London, WC1V7AA, England

Thomas Nelson Australia
102 Dodds Street
South Melbourne 3205
Victoria, Australia

Nelson Canada
1120 Birchmount Road
Scarborough, Ontario M1K 5G4, Canada

16 15 14 13 12 11 10 9 8 7 6 5 4 3

Library of Congress Cataloging-in-Publication Data

VanDyke, Scott, 1954-
    From line to design: design graphics communication / Scott
VanDyke. — 3rd ed.
        p.   cm.
    Includes bibliographical references.
    ISBN 0-442-00113-4
    1. Communication in design.   I. Title
NK1510.V28   1990
741.6--dc20
                                        89-70627
                                        CIP

Contents

Preface

This book has evolved out of a personal interest in design/graphics, and a personal frustration with the frequent separation of the two in the environmental design curriculum.

Typically, students starting out in environmental design take basic graphics courses which concentrate on technical drafting skills and refined illustrative graphic technique. At the same time, these students are also enrolled in basic design courses that concentrate on abstract and conceptual design thinking and theory.

Confusion results when students are told on the one hand to visually communicate design ideas in illustrative detail, but at the same time are told to disregard detail and think abstractly. To eliminate this confusion, basic graphics and design courses should be at the same level of instruction; moreover, the interdependency of the two should not be divided, but rather united in a collaborative approach to design development. The objective of this book is to suggest such an approach and provide exercises for the design student to explore design-graphics relationships.

It would be foolish to suggest that the techniques discussed in this book are the only ways to approach environmental design, but when understood and applied, these techniques may prove to be an asset in developing design ideas quickly and effectively.

The information presented in this book is based on the observations, literature and personal design-graphics experiences that relate to landscape architecture and environmental design. Hopefully those who opt to scan the pages of this book will benefit from the ideas presented and work to develop their own approach.

Exercise 1: FROM LINE TO DESIGN

Place a sheet of tracing paper over this page and, beginning at number
1 in the lower left-hand corner connect all the points.

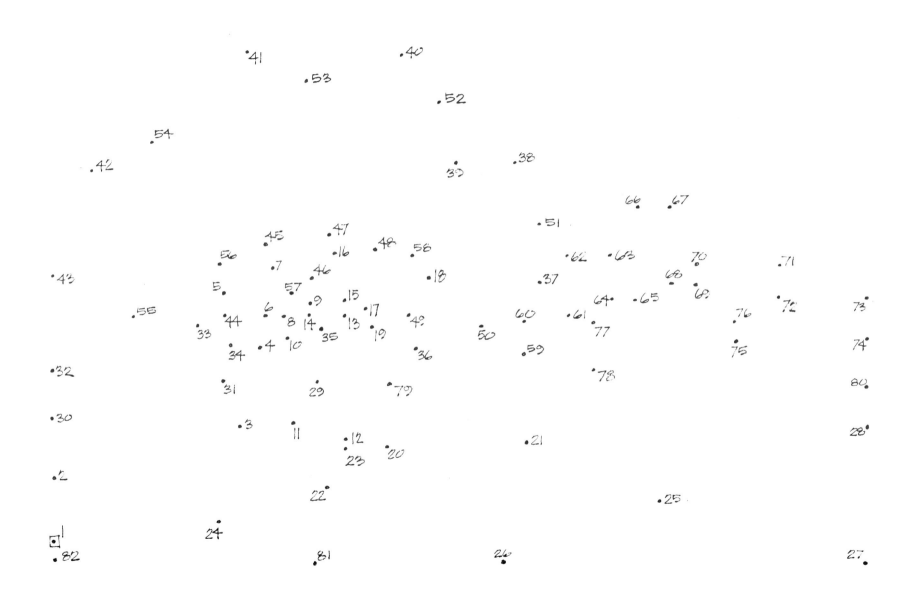

Introduction

DESIGN-GRAPHICS COMMUNICATION RELATIONSHIP

Upon completion of the first exercise, you have in essence demonstrated the design-graphics communication approach: using graphics to communicate design ideas. This statement and exercise is obviously an oversimplification of a sometimes complex subject. Nevertheless it does serve to illustrate the design-graphics relationship which is the focus of this book. Perhaps this relationship can better be described by defining its primary elements.

Design is problem solving. It involves a cyclical, yet progressive process of evaluation, synthesis, and refinement of design ideas. Designing is not however, simply entering in information and having a solution spew out. It is like a creative battle that is often won or lost in the initial stages of the struggle. Good design relies on solid and well-organized concepts to insure victory. These concepts are the result of the cyclical process that is fundamental to design problem solving.

Graphics is the visualization of the design process, from conception to completion. It provides the means by which you can more effectively evaluate, synthesize, and refine your ideas. It represents an integral part of design, not an end product. There are various levels of graphics in the design process, just as there are various levels of design ideas. The application of each of these levels is related to the level of the refinement of those ideas.

synthesis
refinement
Design Process
evaluation

Visualization of design ideas

The significance of the design-graphics relationship is that it enables the *communication* of your ideas quickly and effectively. Many people, including yourself, who are involved in the design process, are better able to understand and develop their ideas if they are able to communicate these ideas graphically. In other words, don't say it, portray it. A simple diagram may help to illustrate this point.

The concept of design being a battle that is won or lost in the initial stages of the struggle should be extended to suggest that this struggle can be lessened by applying this relationship to the overall design development. This book is an attempt to help you understand these relationships and apply them to your own design efforts.

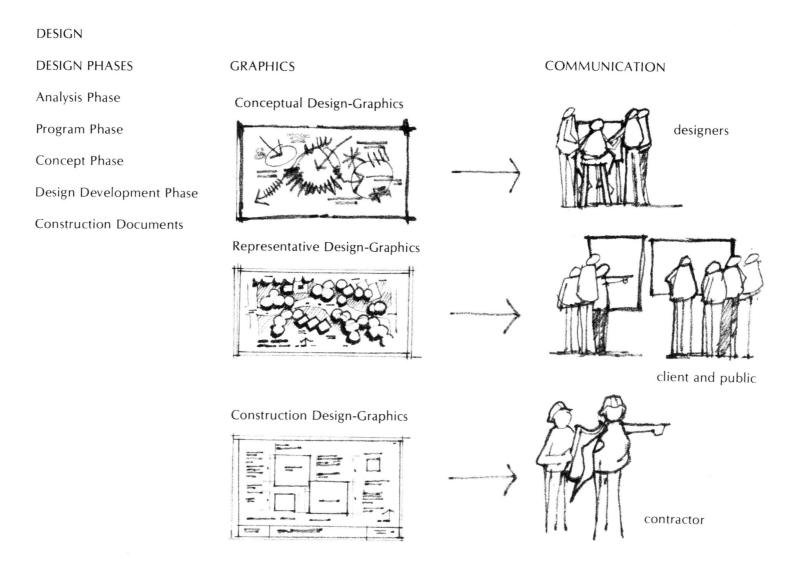

DESIGN

DESIGN PHASES

Analysis Phase

Program Phase

Concept Phase

Design Development Phase

Construction Documents

GRAPHICS

Conceptual Design-Graphics

Representative Design-Graphics

Construction Design-Graphics

COMMUNICATION

designers

client and public

contractor

How to Use This Book

This book is not a text. It is not a complete or even partial authority on the subject of design and graphics. It has been prepared to act as a supplement to other design-graphics texts, and aid in design-graphics instruction.

Many of the terms used in the book may be unfamiliar to you, or alterations of terms you have seen elsewhere. Many are new terms developed simply for the organization of this book. The terminology however, is not as important as the ideas represented.

In order to gain a full understanding of the design-graphics communication relationships, you must apply them. There is a series of exercises included in this book to help you develop this understanding. You will need a supply of tracing paper, pencils or pens, your eyes, your hands and your mind to complete these exercises. Use the tracing paper to work the exercises as many times or ways that you desire. Do your work freehand, unless the instructions state otherwise, and try to increase your speed as well as your ability to communicate your ideas graphically. Be bold, be courageous and explore the opportunities of design-graphics communication. Not everyone will be on the same level of proficiency, but everyone can work on improving.

The exercises provided here are very generally stated, and are presented as examples of the type of exercises that could be created for developing design-graphics understanding and ability.

Practice. The best way to develop your abilities in design-graphics communications is to continually work at it.

SECTION A
CONCEPTUAL DESIGN-GRAPHICS

The first section of discussion and exercises is an introduction to the fundamental and abstract characteristics of the design-graphics relationship. "Conceptual" design-graphics refers to the level of graphic communications used in the initial stages of the design process.

Little, if any, consideration is made in this section for refinement or detail. In beginning the design process you are only interested in analytical and conceptual ideation. Refinement, therefore, is needed only to the extent that you as a designer want to visualize your conceptual ideas for personal evaluation or the evaluation of other designers. Remember, when doing the exercises in this section, disregard detail and concentrate your efforts on developing ideas.

1

Abstract Images I

The environment is composed of objects and actions that in combination create the tangible, dimensional, and visual world in which we live. In our efforts to modify and design the environment, it is important to understand the basic elements and principles upon which this design is founded.

The first step to this understanding is the removal of detail from the environment and the observation of things as abstract images. For example, with the use of abstract imagery, buildings, vegetation, or relationships, are converted to abstract forms and symbols. Simplification of the environment in this way enables you to evaluate these elements without becoming overwhelmed with specifics, and enhances the opportunity to identify fundamental design elements and principles. This section examines various abstract elements and principles that you should understand and apply in your design-graphics.

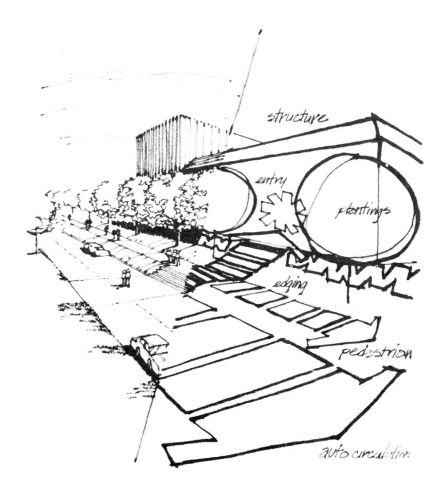

DESIGN ELEMENTS

If you cue your mind to think in simple, geometric terms for a moment, you might define the environment using several "design elements." For example, you could say that the environment is composed of many points which in combination create lines. Lines combine to create planes of shape, which unite to become volumes of form, and the void remaining is called "space."

These design elements are the fundamental building blocks for most of the abstract images that will be discussed in this chapter. Other design elements that are important in formulating the environment are value, texture and color. Understanding these basic elements and utilizing them in developing your conceptual design-graphics will help you become a more conscientious designer.

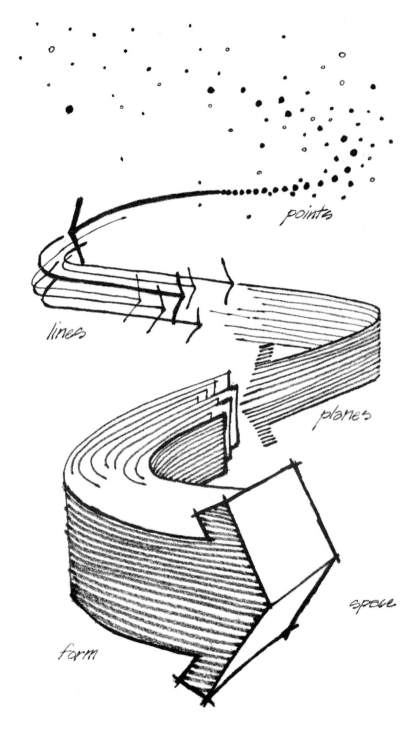

points

lines

planes

form

space

Line

Quick and meaningful use of line is essential to design-graphics communication. Initially you think of line as being an edge or an outline, but line can be extended to describe a variety of other elements. It is the basis for most graphic communications.

Like many aspects of the design process, line has a variety of levels of refinement and meaning. The first few exercises will explore the various uses of line and the importance of line control, which is simply drawing line with a conscientious effort to make the line communicate the appropriate meaning and intention. Line control, a skill based on eye-hand relationships and continual practice, suggests the delineator knows what lines to use and why, and how to portray them effectively.

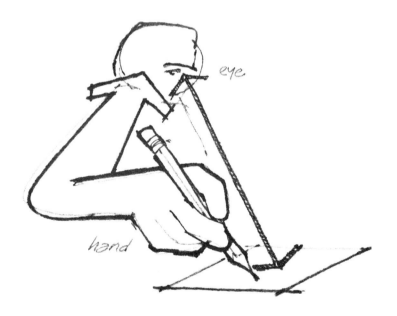

Straight Line. The straight line is the most simple and basic line, but often the most difficult to draw free-hand. Those who have trouble drawing straight lines may want to try looking to where the line will terminate rather than at the line itself. In order to do this, you may have to shift your hand position slightly or shift the position of the paper. Begin slowly, then increase your speed at drawing straight lines, while maintaining line control.

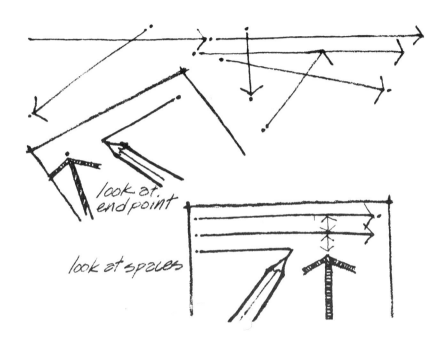

Parallel Line. Now that you can draw straight lines between points, how well can you draw straight lines parallel to each other? Again drawing parallel lines will require good eye-hand control. For those who would like another hint, try looking at the space between the lines, rather than the line. Your eye is a fairly good judge of proportions.

Start slowly, and increase your speed as you feel confident. Maintain line control.

Expressive Line. Variations of lines (direction, weight, angle, etc.) are often used to suggest various emotions and meanings. For example, vertical, bold, straight lines, suggest strength and support while horizontal, thin, undulating lines suggest serenity and calm. Examine the lines in the examples and consider the structure of the line as it relates to the expression. Then try line variations of your own to express different emotions and meaning. As a follow-up exercise, redraw Exercise No. 1 using expressive lines, and evaluate the result.

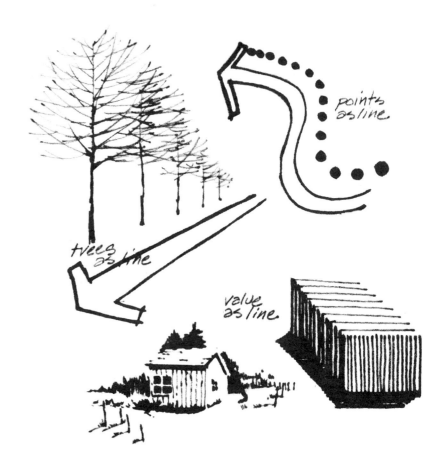

sweeping

gaiety

tension

impact

electric

calm

sporatic

Implied Line. Often line is created or suggested without the actual physical appearance of an edge or outline. For example, a row of trees may imply a line or boundary, points in close proximity may communicate a line, or contrasts between values may create an edge or line. Implied lines are useful in all aspects of actual design development as well as design-graphics communication. Become familiar with the properties and potentials of implied line as an important design element.

Curved Line. Curved lines, like straight and parallel lines, are basic but difficult to draw. Apply the suggestions for straight-line technique to curved lines, but try to keep your hands and fingers fluid and flowing with the curves. Practice will undoubtedly improve your line control and speed.

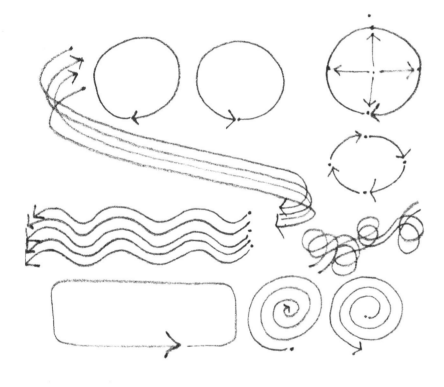

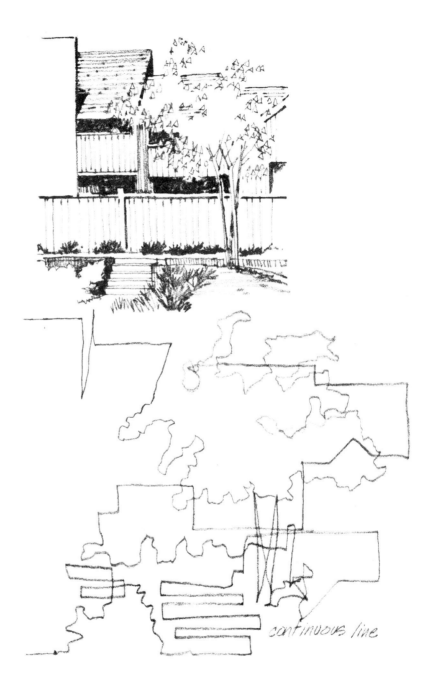

continuous line

Continuous Line. An interesting way to evaluate your eye-hand control, is to draw continuous, or contour line drawings. Without looking at your paper, draw an object by continually looking at it. Move slowly and patiently. Don't worry about lines that double over or feel awkward, just maintain eye contact with the object and pencil contact with your paper. Results of a conscientious effort will produce a line drawing with meaning and character.

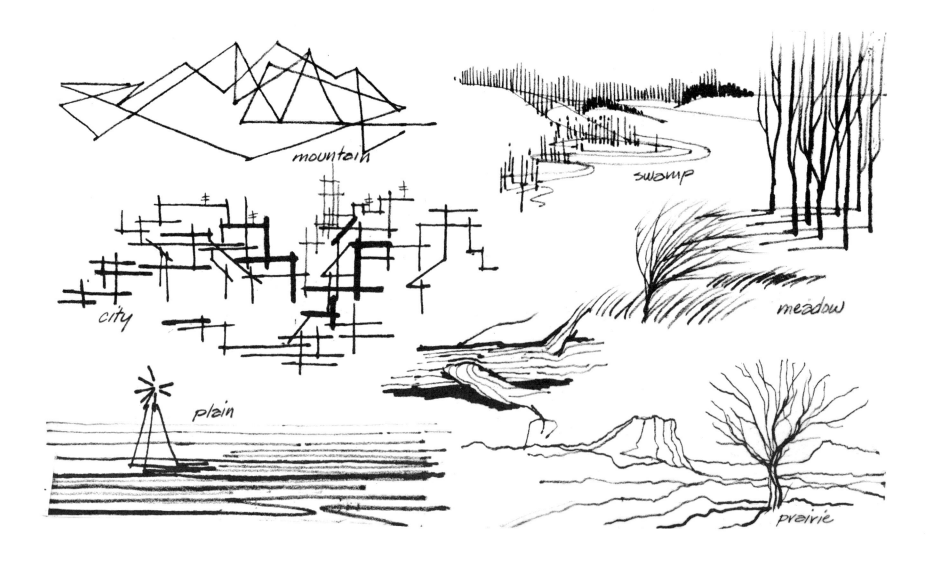

mountain

swamp

city

meadow

plain

prairie

Line in the Environment. To help you understand the environment, evaluate and consider the various lines suggested in the examples shown above and notice the abstract characteristics of line in relation to the actual image. So you can more easily define these lines, concentrate on the abstract imagery by squinting your eyes a little or blur your vision in order to observe the details.

Exercise 2: LINE

a. Draw a series of straight and parallel lines as indicated in the examples.

b. Trace the examples of curved lines and circles, then try a series of connecting curved lines between points.

c. Select an element in the environment, a chair, tree, etc., and draw the image with continuous line. Remember to look only at the object and not your paper. Try to feel your hand moving over the object.

d. Draw lines that express the following: hate, fear, sleep, excitement, surprise, rhythm, war, solitude, flight, success, suspense, and others of your choice.

e. Examine photographs to identify the presence of actual or implied line, and trace the image using only those lines.

f. Create abstract line images for the following environmental settings: farm, zoo, amusement park, canyon, coastline, and others of your choice.

Photo by Theodore D. Walker

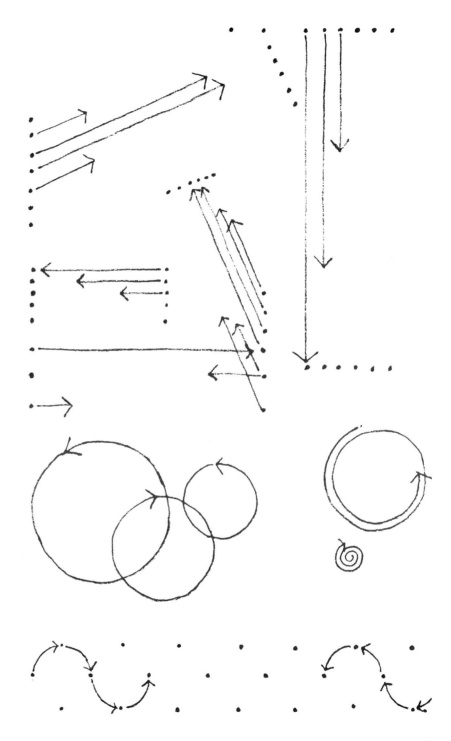

9

Photo by Theodore D. Walker

Photo by Theodore D. Walker

Shapes

By examining some of your work in the line exercises you will undoubtedly begin to see line take on characteristics of shape and form. As you continue to develop a sense for the three-dimensional environment, it is necessary that you understand the two-dimensional qualities that create it.

In the final exercises of the line you were asked to represent a three-dimensional image by simple use of line. If you analyze the results of that exercise more clearly, you will see that there is also a variety of two-dimensional shapes that interrelate to create the image.

In the design-graphics process it is often necessary to communicate ideas two dimensionally, as simple shape or line. This enables an evaluation of the ideas on a simple and abstract level.

Geometric and Organic Shapes. The most basic shapes may be described as "geometric." They include the square, the circle, the rectangle, and the triangle. Artists often use these shapes to "block in" a desired drawing. In this way they are able to quickly and easily evaluate the drawing in terms of proportion and scale.

blocking in images

Many shapes in the natural environment are not square or rounded, however, but irregular or organic. As the design process develops, you should also analyze the design elements of these shapes in relationship to the overall design.

Evaluate the examples of geometric and organic shapes used in describing the images on the next few pages and notice how their relationships are supportive of the design.

11

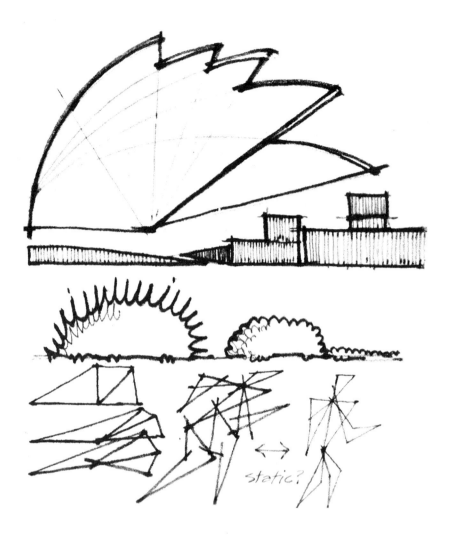

Positive and Negative Shape. In developing your understanding of the environment, it is often helpful to describe physical objects as positive shapes, and the area about the object as negative shapes. Another approach, is to describe the dark and the light variations in shape as positive and negative. After studying the examples, try to define other shapes of the environment in terms of positive and negative.

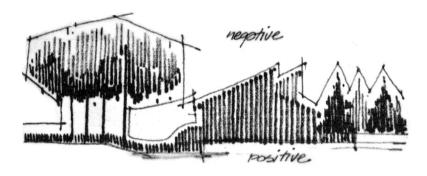

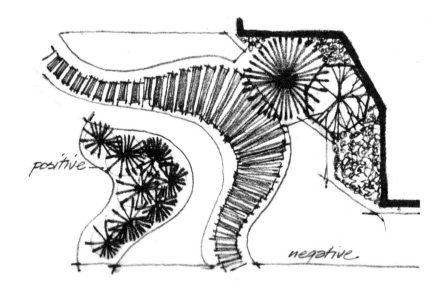

Static or Dynamic Shape. As you evaluate shapes you will discover that they, like lines, have expressive characteristics. Static shapes are those that appear to be at rest or without movement, while dynamic shapes have characteristics suggesting instability or motion. Evaluate the shapes in the preceding examples and analyze the characteristics that produce the image. Notice that the amount of expression in the shape is directly related to the amount of expression in line.

12

Implied Shape and Dividing Shape. Often there are examples of shape that have no definite limits or boundaries, but are merely implied. Like implied line, these shapes may be described by various cues that suggest shape. For example, an enclosure of trees may imply a shape, or a succession of lines may create shape, or they may be defined by the contrasts of shapes, as in the juxtaposition of positive and negative shapes.

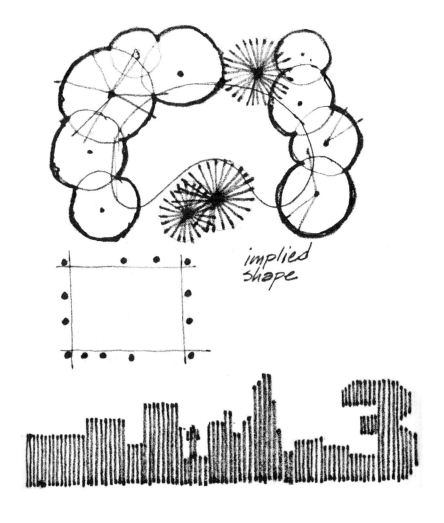

implied shape

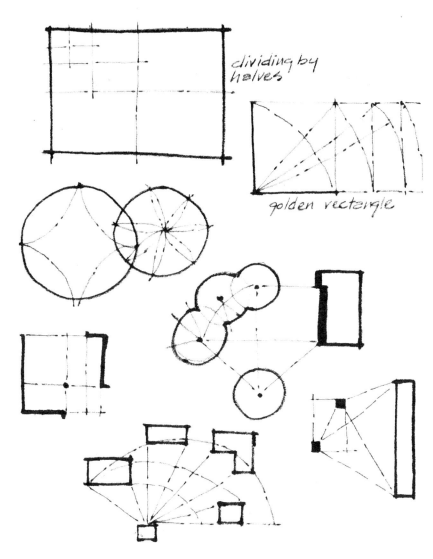

dividing by halves

golden rectangle

Another approach to defining shape is to divide a basic shape into component shapes. The technique is similar to drawing implied shapes, in that often there are cues as to how the division might occur. Other times the division may be based on geometric calculations or may simply be an experimental approach. Evaluate the techniques used in the examples and notice the cues that help to suggest the divisions.

13

Exercise 3: SHAPE

a. Examine photographs to identify abstract shapes and planes.

b. Create environmental images using only geometric or only organic shapes.

c. Use simple geometric shapes to create static or dynamic shapes.

d. Examine photographs to identify various examples of positive or negative shape.

e. Develop other shapes from the examples given, by creating implied shapes or by dividing the shape.

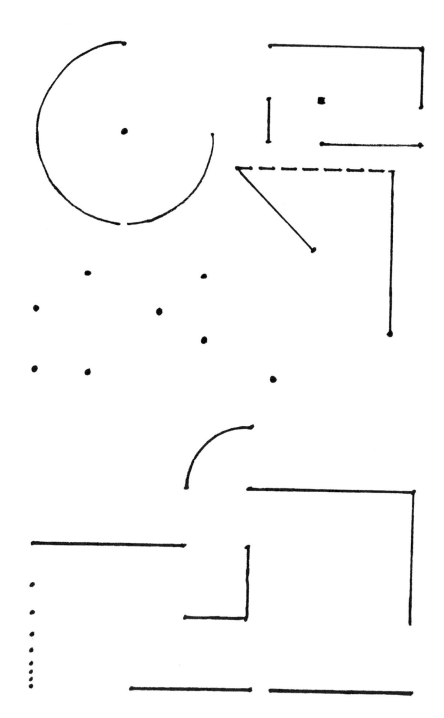

Photo by Theodore D. Walker

Photos by Theodore D. Walker

16

Photo by Theodore D. Walker

Form and Space

A design element that is very important, especially when related to environmental design, is "form." Form in design represents the aspect of volume and three-dimensions—length, width, and depth. In designing and developing the three-dimensional environment in which we live, the ability to understand, utilize and communicate form is essential.

An equally important element directly related to form and the environment is "space." Often the term is used exclusively to describe various aspects of the environment. You will undoubtedly hear designers speak of the quality and purpose of the space in evaluating design ideas. You should become familiar with this type of evaluation.

17

Isometric Form and Space. The term "isometric form and space" is more overpowering in appearance than it is in actuality. It is simply a three-dimensional method for describing form and space. If one identifies the various geometric shapes in the environment and then develops them to represent an isometric form (see "paraline," Chapter 3), one can easily visualize the three-dimensional qualities. The examples and exercises will help you understand this valuable technique portraying three-dimensional forms.

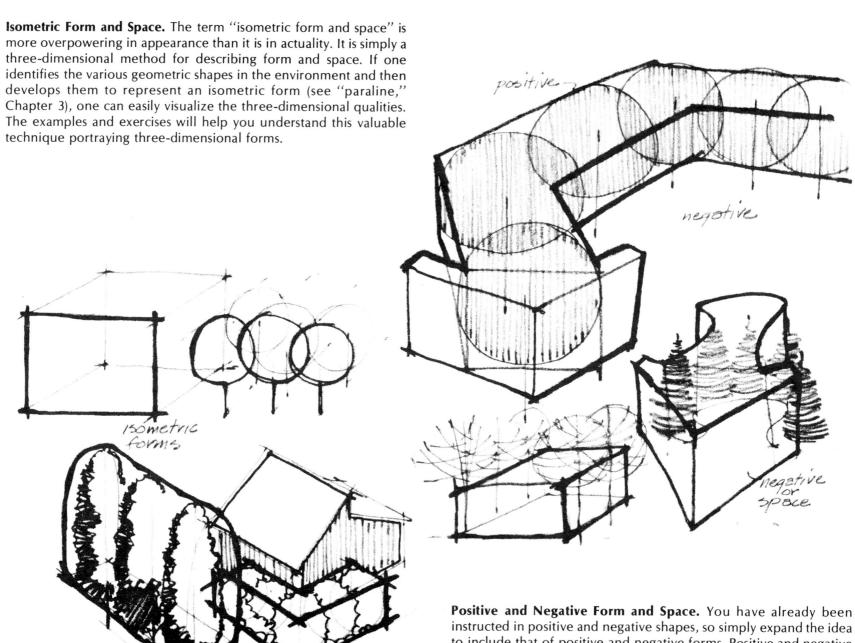

isometric forms

positive

negative

negative or space

Positive and Negative Form and Space. You have already been instructed in positive and negative shapes, so simply expand the idea to include that of positive and negative forms. Positive and negative forms are three-dimensional representations of positive and negative shapes. Often these terms are intermixed with the idea of space. You will probably begin speaking in terms of positive and negative space as you evaluate your design ideas.

Exercise 4: FORM and SPACE

a. Draw three-dimensional images from the examples given by creating isometric forms.

b. Examine photographs and identify the presence of form and space.

c. Identify the examples of positive or negative form or space that may be present in various photographs of the environment.

d. Identify the cues that create the actual or implied, positive or negative forms and space.

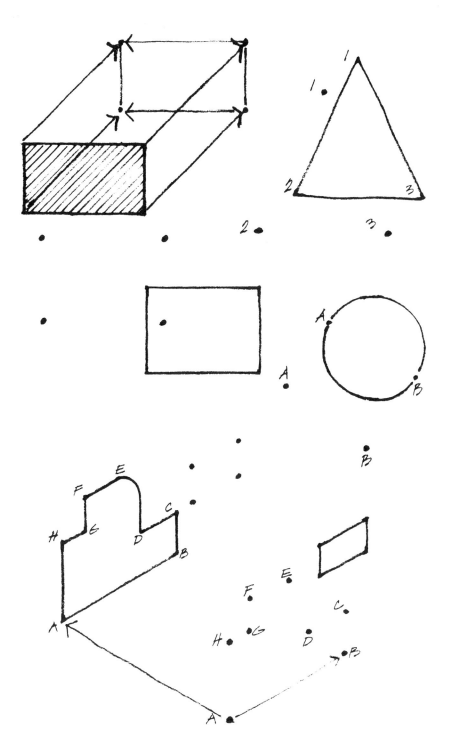

Photo by Theodore D. Walker

Photos by Theodore D. Walker

21

Texture

Another important design element to understand and utilize is "texture." Texture usually suggests a tactile sensation that accompanies a surface. For example, sandpaper shows a rough or coarse texture when compared to the smooth or fine texture of polished marble.

Comparisons of the textural characteristics of objects are a fundamental part of understanding and applying texture to design. The same sandpaper, for instance, may be described as having a fine texture when compared to the coarseness of a cobblestone road.

In the environment there are numberous examples of textures and textural relationships. The size and shapes of the foliage on plants may describe various textures and tactile sensations.

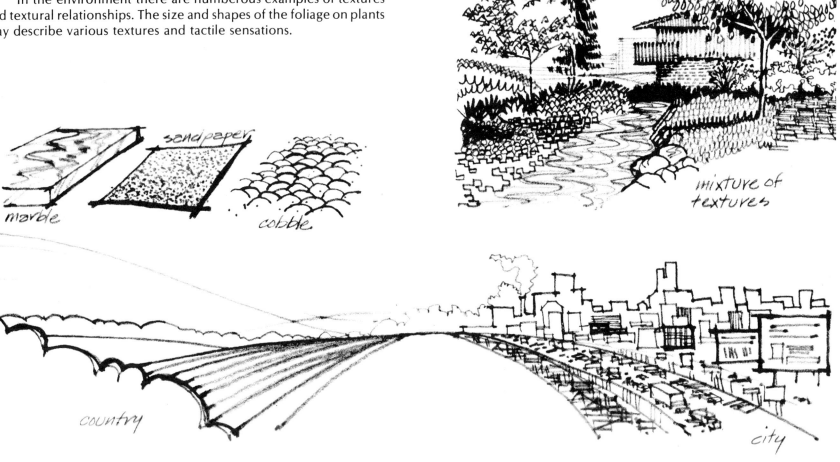

marble

sandpaper

cobble

mixture of textures

country

city

Value and Color

Two final elements of design that are also effective in creating the environment are value and color. Value refers to the relationship of lightness and darkness, and color to the hue or reflective characteristic of light. Understanding the effects of light on the environment is very important to the development of environmental design ideas. In this book, however, most of the information is related to value, with very little mention of color.

Value is directly related to the other design elements in that it further describes their basic characteristics. For example, a three-dimensional form is more easily defined by the utilization of different values or tones. Shade and shadow (see Chapter 7) are very significant in determining our perception of the environment, and perhaps ultimate behavior in the environment. A dark, heavily shadowed design, for example, may invite a particular type of user behavior.

Exercise 5: TEXTURE and VALUE

a. Do rubbings on various surfaces to produce textures and patterns.

b. Use basic design elements to develop textural images for the following environmental elements: vegetation foliage, gravel, brick, grass, cobblestone, shingle, sand, water, concrete and others of your choice.

c. Apply values of line or texture to the examples given to help identify the planes.

d. Return to the preceding exercises in shape, form and space and apply values of line and texture to your drawings.

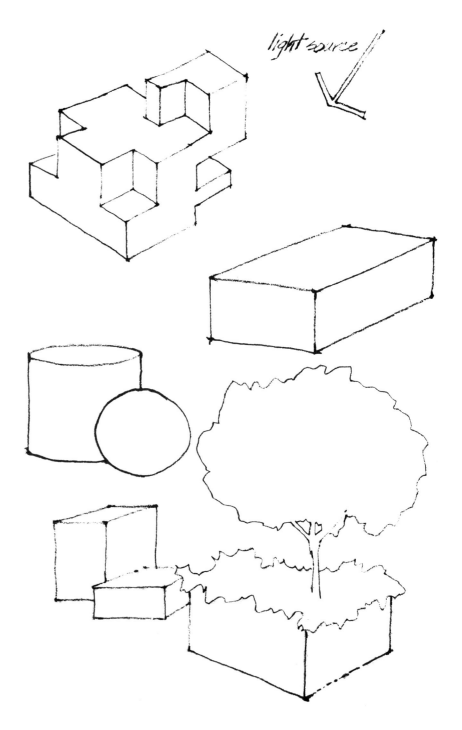

light source

DESIGN PRINCIPLES

The principles of unity, balance and emphasis are often used to organize and structure the elements to create a complete or whole design. With these principles in mind the designer can develop a design solution that has both form and function.

The design principles, like the elements, are fundamental in character, but provide the basis for development of design ideas. Understanding these characteristics will help you develop a sense for the structure and relationships of many of the design elements. Also, like the elements, design principles are rarely used individually, each usually working with, or supporting the other. For purposes of suggesting the use of design principles as approaches to effective design problem solving, however, consider each separately and evaluate the various techniques for applying them to the design process.

Unity

Unity suggests an overall togetherness in design; it is the fabric about which the entire design is interwoven. Unity is a means by which order can be maintained among the elements. In designs that lack unity the elements compete for dominance causing chaos. In the environment there are numerous examples of the absence of unity both in function and appearance resulting in an increased amount of anxiety and confusion.

The application of the principle of unity is significant in all aspects of the design-graphics relationship. As you proceed through this book, and in your design curriculum, seek to develop your understanding of unity and the various techniques that can help create it.

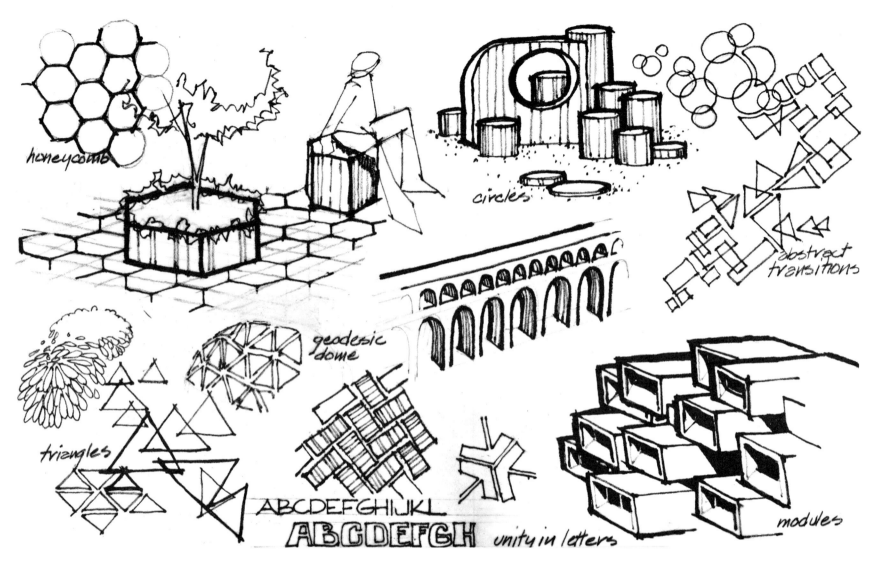

honeycomb

circles

abstract transitions

geodesic dome

triangles

ABCDEFGHIJKL
ABCDEFGH unity in letters

modules

Repetition. One approach to establishing unity in a design is to repeat the basic elements. In past exercises you noticed that much of the work done simply with line or squares maintains an overall unified character.

While observing the examples above, you should evaluate the use of repetition in creating unity and then apply the principles to the exercises that follow. Notice that the more complex or varied the elements, the more difficult it is to maintain unity. Therefore, keep in mind the fact that simplicity helps maintain unity.

Module and Grid. The modular approach to unity is similar to repetition. By using a single modular shape and combining or dividing it, you are able to maintain a unified character throughout the design.

The grid, another method to create unity, is very similar to the modular and repetition methods. The grid is based on the division of shapes into a uniform and continuous pattern of squares or rectangles.

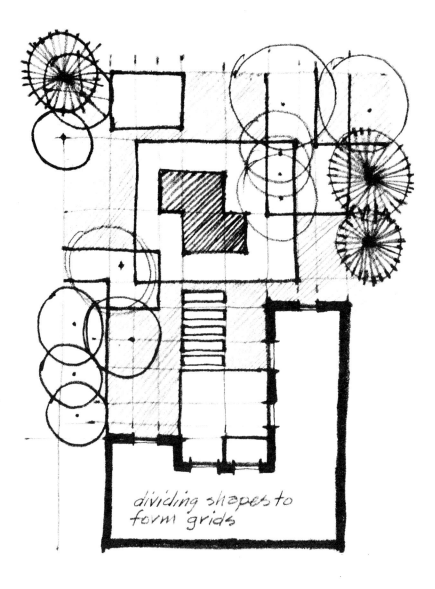

dividing shapes to form grids

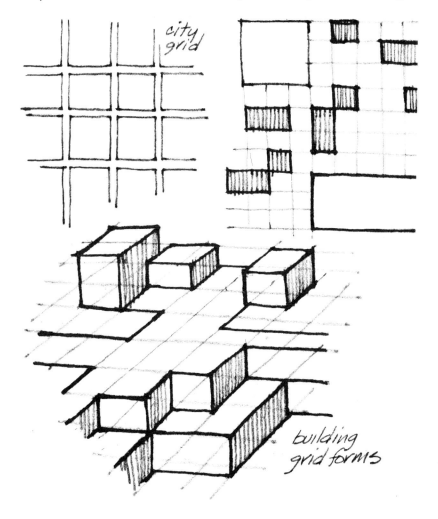

city grid

building grid forms

Theme. Unity is like a thread that weaves throughout the design holding it together. Often as a mechanism for developing design and maintaining unity, it is possible to create a theme or meaning for the design. You have undoubtedly heard of a "theme park" for example. In the following examples notice how the lines, shapes, and form all relate to the overall themes indicated.

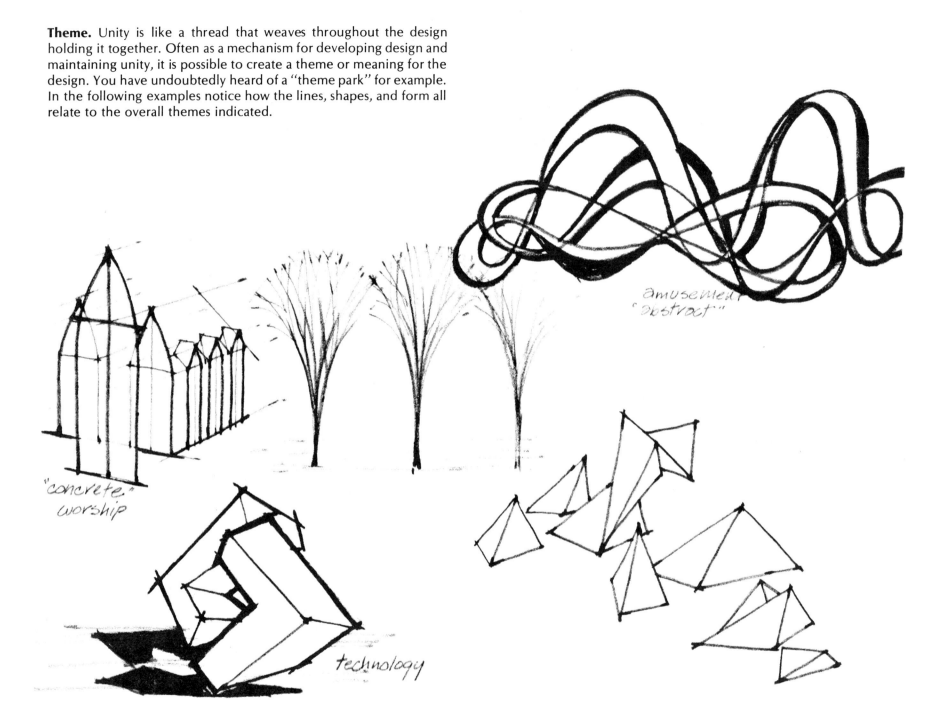

"concrete" worship

amusement "abstract"

technology

Exercise 6: UNITY

a. Select a basic design element such as a line, shape, or form, from the examples to the right, and repeatedly trace it. Evaluate the images that result. Notice the positive, negative, implied and actual aspects that are created. Also notice whether or not the image appears to "hang together."

b. Divide the example given into a grid, and identify various modules that result.

c. Create abstracts or images that portray the following themes: defense, academia, wilderness, technology, athletics, space exploration, frontier, jungle, Stone Age and others of your choice. Consider the various elements that make up each theme.

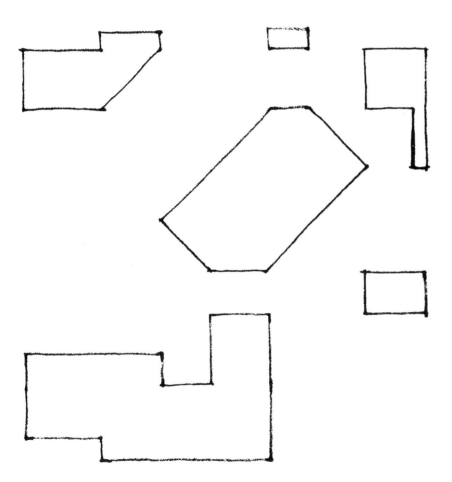

Balance

Another fundamental principle in design development is balance. Balance suggests equilibrium in the design and thereby increases the opportunities for order and unity. Balance in most instances is not, however, as easily measured as placing weights on a scale. It is related to a variety of different design elements and other design principles which complicate the perception of balance in design, especially when applied to environmental settings.

A very important judge of balance is the eye. If the eye perceives the design as balanced and unified, then that is usually sufficient. There are no particular rules for creating balance, only a number of approaches that may help to establish it.

29

A more difficult, but certainly more extensive approach to balance, is asymmetry. Asymetrical balance is more informal in character and, as the name suggests, is not symmetrical. Most of the work done up to this point will undoubtedly represent examples of asymmetrical balance. Quick evaluations of these examples will give you a sense for whether the works are balanced or not. Again, the eye is a fairly good judge of balance.

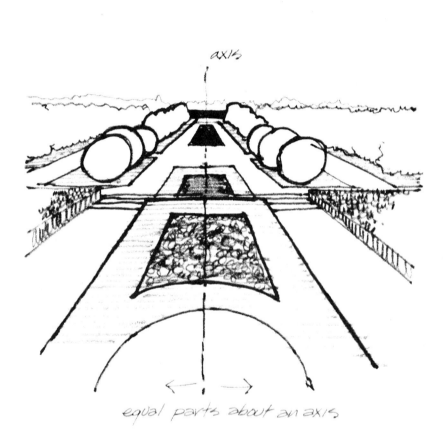

equal parts about an axis

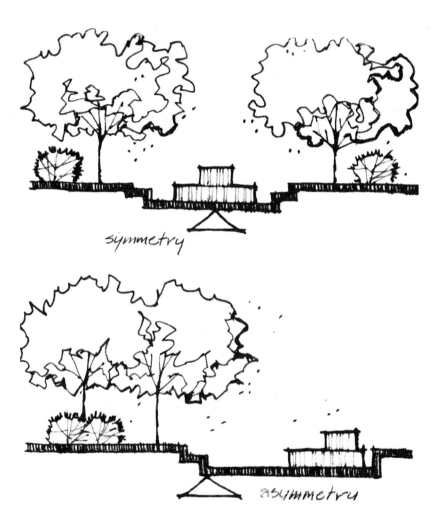

symmetry

asymmetry

Symmetry. If you were to divide your face down the center, each half would be almost identical to the other; your face represents symmetrical balance. If you were to divide a cube in half and then half again, each quarter would resemble the other, the cube is a symmetrical form. Symmetry is a formal example of balance since equal parts are arranged about an axis. It is a simple way to achieve balance when the occasion presents itself and is used quite often.

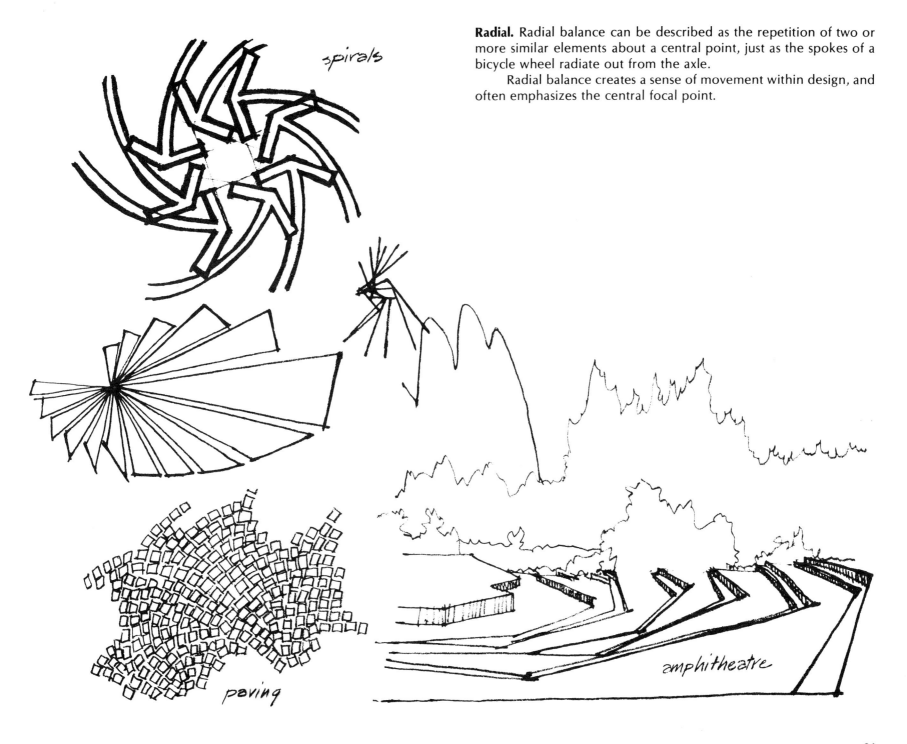

spirals

Radial. Radial balance can be described as the repetition of two or more similar elements about a central point, just as the spokes of a bicycle wheel radiate out from the axle.

Radial balance creates a sense of movement within design, and often emphasizes the central focal point.

spirals

paving

amphitheatre

Exercise 7: BALANCE

a. Using your drawings from the prior exercise on "unity," evaluate the presence of "balance" in the images.

b. Evaluate drawings of designed or natural environments and check the "balance" of the design elements.

c. Organize the shapes to the right into images displaying symmetrical, asymmetrical, and radial balance.

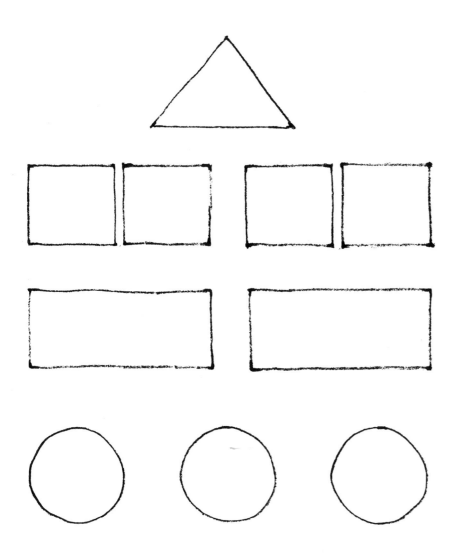

Emphasis

The discussion of radial balance described the creation of a focal point by radiating shapes about an axis. Often this focal point defines the emphasis of a design. The principle of emphasis, like balance and unity, helps to create order within a design by organizing the elements as a whole.

If some elements or aspects of a design are more important than others those elements should be emphasized. Through the use of this principle you can produce a design with variety but not competition.

Remember to evaluate emphasis in relationship to the other principles already discussed. In this way you will be building upon your understanding of design and be more able to apply this principle to your own design work.

Directionality. If you examine your work in the radial balance exercise, as well as other exercises, you will notice that the lines, shapes, and forms will often direct your eye to various parts of the work. These elements virtually point the observer in the desired direction, creating emphasis. Some directionality may be more obvious than others. Some may be obvious to the point of being overbearing. As you complete the directionality exercises, evaluate the results and decide what characteristics make it subtle, obvious, or overbearing.

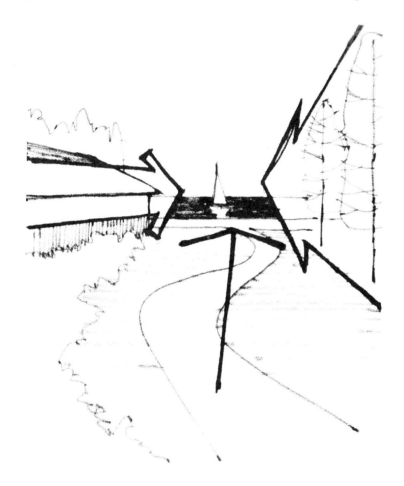

Placement and Contrast. The placement of an element relative to other elements can also create emphasis. In the accompanying examples, evaluate the strengths and subtleties of results in the placement of elements.

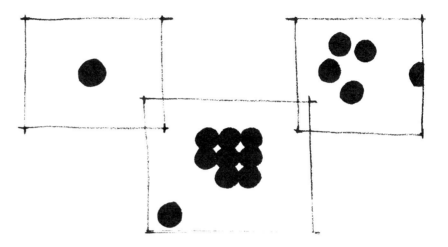

Contrasting elements is another approach to creating emphasis. Contrasts in line, shape, or form, and contrasts in value, or texture are also effective techniques.

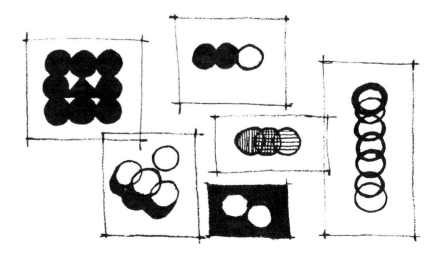

33

Another simple technique for emphasizing elements, is to increase or decrease the number of the elements used. Notice how these techniques, as many others, are often related to and build upon one another. Also notice the relationship between the number and the intensity of the emphasis.

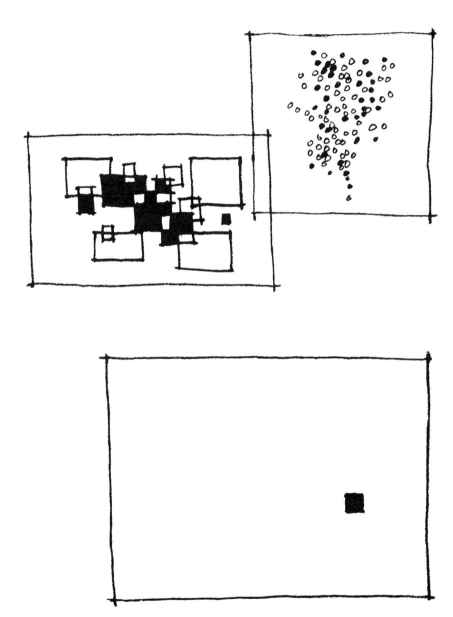

Size and Number. By varying the sizes of the elements in the design, you can also create emphasis. Again it should be apparent that the more intense the variation, the more obvious the emphasis. You may want to consider, however, which of the elements, large or small, is the element that receives the greatest emphasis.

Exercise 8: EMPHASIS

a. Evaluate the elements in drawings of designed or natural environments and locate the focal point. What aspects of the image create the emphasis?

b. Use simple design elements—line, shape or form, to create a series of abstract images that direct emphasis to a focal point.

c. Use the results of previous exercises or newly-created images to produce areas of emphasis by contrasting the elements.

d. Vary the size, number or placement of various elements in your images to create interest and emphasis.

2

Abstract Images II

ENVIRONMENTAL ELEMENTS

In developing your understanding of the design-graphics process, it will be helpful for you to become acquainted with "environmental elements." Although these elements are still abstract in their imagery, they begin to categorize more concrete aspects of the environment (see Lynch, *Image of the City*). Many of them are used by various environmental design professions and provide a basis for both graphic and verbal communication of design ideas.

The exercises presented on the following pages are intended to give you a basic understanding of these elements, and suggest methods to portray them graphically. It is important that you continue to expand your knowledge and use of the design-graphics techniques presented here, as well as all the other techniques in the book.

Paths

One of the most fundamental environmental elements, combines many aspects of movement into a category called "paths." Paths, in a very general sense, can include anything from physical circulation/transportation modes, to abstract relationships. In most instances paths are represented graphically by arrows. In the following examples you should evaluate the use of paths, and then develop examples of your own based on the information given. Notice that the abstract design elements and principles used to communicate paths, have a strong bearing on their meaning and interpretation.

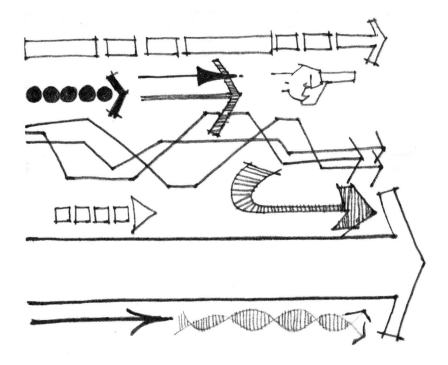

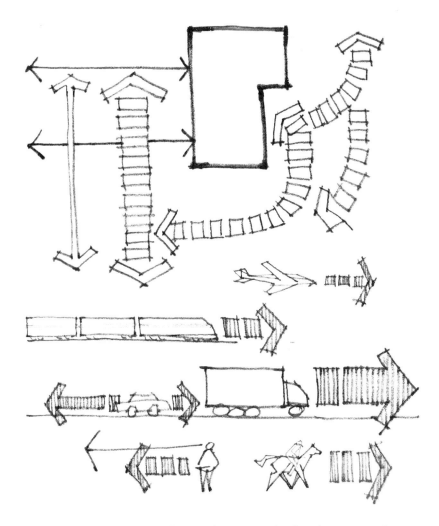

Circulation/Transportation. When one thinks about circulation/transportation paths, undoubtedly visions of cars, trucks, planes and people appear. In the environment there is a multitude of these types of paths, plus many others. The circulation and transportation of air, water and minerals are examples of other circulating transportation paths. The circulation of heat or the reflection of the sun's rays are also examples of paths often considered in the development of design ideas.

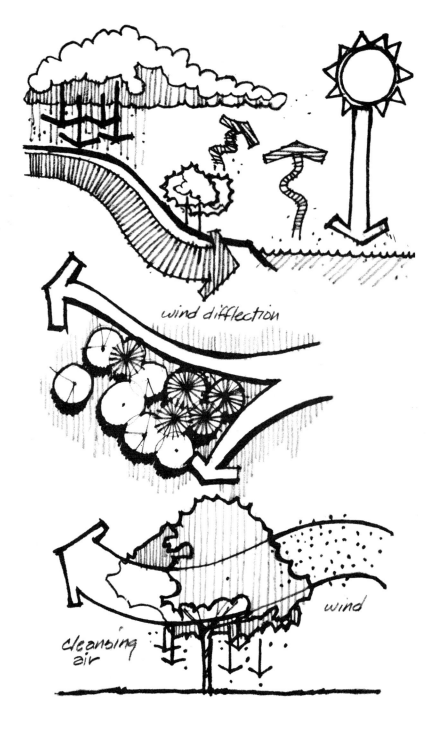

wind difflection

cleansing
air

wind

Relationships. Paths in the environment have movement, not only in the physical sense, but also in relationship to one another. For example, a children's play area and an elementary school have a strong attractive relationship to one another, similar to the influence of a magnetic force and steel. Paths can also suggest progressive relationships or sequences of ideas, such as information describing methodology or procedure.

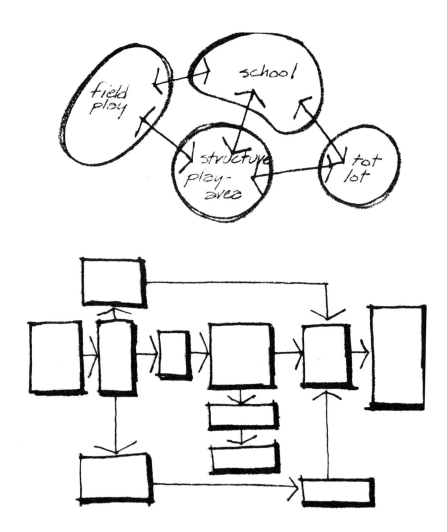

Nodes

Other environmental elements that have special significance are called "nodes." Nodes suggest that a certain quality or character of the environment demands special consideration. They are used to describe both positive and negative, abstract and concrete qualities, depending on the application. For example a park fountain may be a positive feature due to its cool, relaxing character, but a negative feature because it poses a hazard to small children.

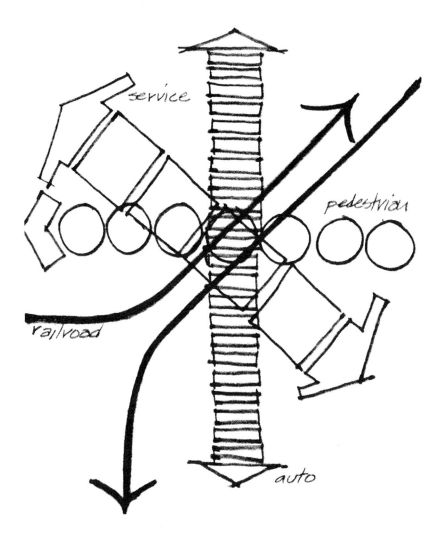

Intersections. One common description of a node is the intersection of paths. Many lanes of traffic converging at a particular point for example, would definitely create some special considerations. These intersections may also suggest entrances and exits, meeting places, coordinated points in time or space, or the convergence of ideas or meanings.

Emphasis/Special Interest Nodes. Some nodes may suggest characteristics of special interest, such as a landmark or historic site. Others may suggest places of emphasis or focus, such as a fountain or a flowering tree. The nodes may also suggest a large area of interest like a neighborhood, community or metropolitan city. The application of the element is relative to the intentions of the designer.

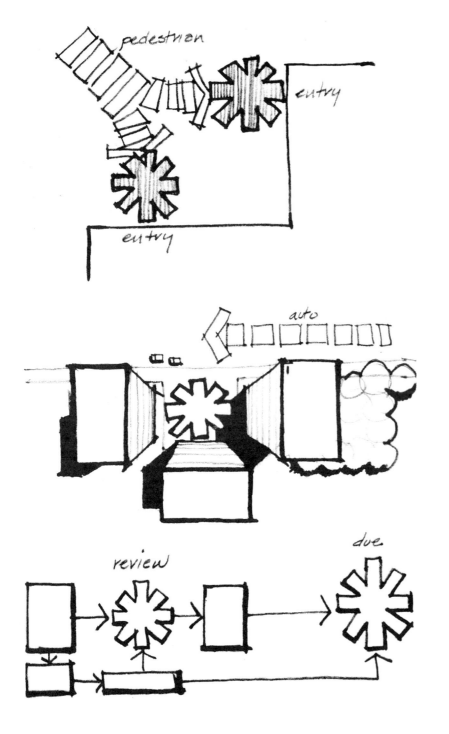

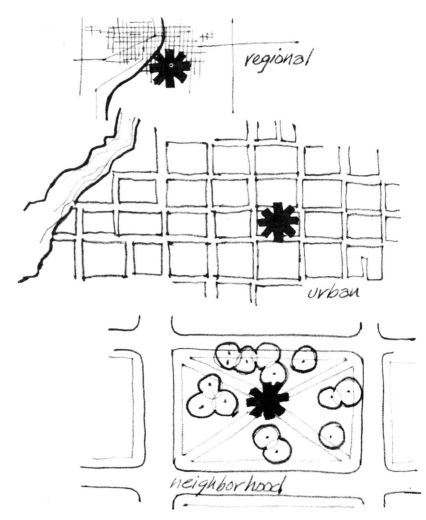

Districts

Often there are elements in the environment that in combination have a particular character or relationship. In defining these areas you may in fact refer to them as an "area," or you may label them as being a "district." Like the node, a district can be large or small, depending on its application to the design intention. In relation to the nodes, however, the district usually describes the foundation elements in which a particular node is located. The small park might represent the district for the previous fountain example.

Function/Relationship. Districts are often easily defined if they have similar functional characteristics. A parking lot, a campus, a city, all have a variety of elements that characterize the function of the space. Other districts are defined by more abstract or psychological relationships, such as socioeconomic or cultural characteristics. A state, a county, a neighborhood, even a country are examples of districts that can be differentiated by these characteristics.

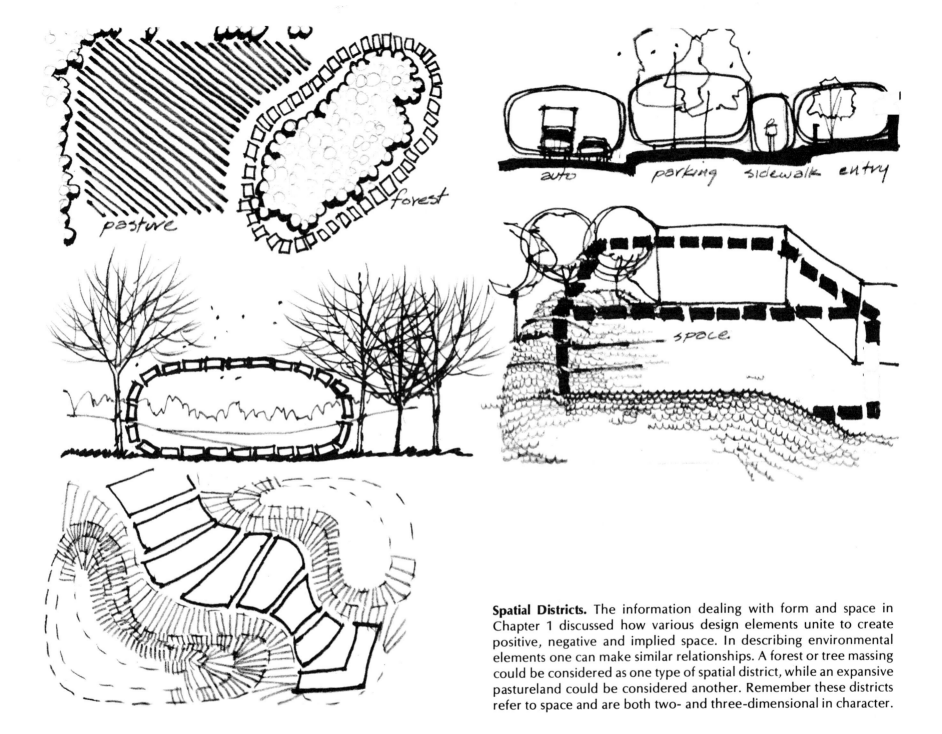

pasture

forest

auto parking sidewalk entry

space.

Spatial Districts. The information dealing with form and space in Chapter 1 discussed how various design elements unite to create positive, negative and implied space. In describing environmental elements one can make similar relationships. A forest or tree massing could be considered as one type of spatial district, while an expansive pastureland could be considered another. Remember these districts refer to space and are both two- and three-dimensional in character.

Edges

Other environmental elements are used to describe characteristics that divide or separate the environment. These are called "edges." Edges can be physical or abstract, and can also combine characteristics of the other environmental elements. They are important in defining the limits and parameters of the other elements. The outermost regions of a district, for instance, suggest the limit of a district and are defined as edges.

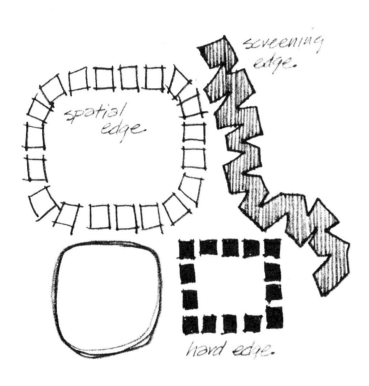

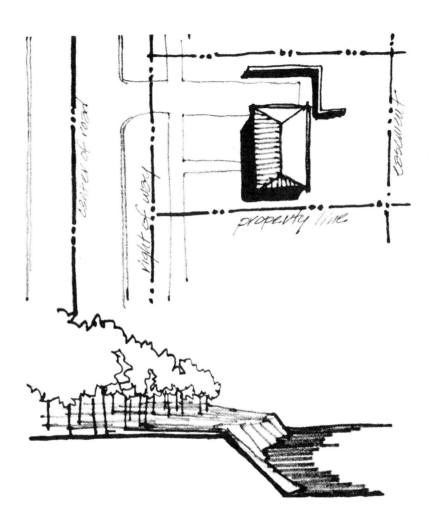

Boundaries and Separation. Many districts have specific edges that define the boundaries of their influence. Property lines, right-of-ways, and easements are examples of abstract edges created by politics or procedure. Other, more physical edges, such as fences, hedgerows and walls, may relate to these boundaries, but their effect is more powerful. A cliff or a water body is an example of a natural edge that separates or screens off aspects of the environment.

Implied Edges. Edges, like line and space, are often simply implied. Some examples of these edges have already been discussed earlier in this section. (See Chapter 1). A significant part of implied edges is the cues that suggest them. They may be cues similar to the ones mentioned for implied shape, or they may represent more abstract cues such as territorial influences and traditional boundaries. Understanding these edges can be extremely important to your design development and ultimate design success.

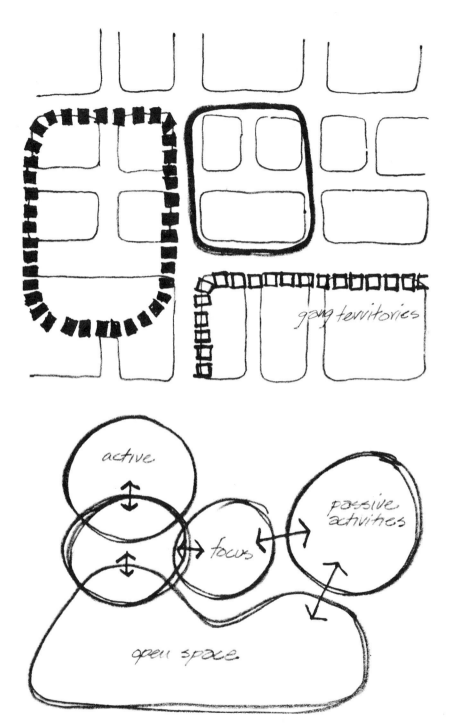

gang territories

Exercise 9: ENVIRONMENTAL ELEMENTS

a. Develop a list of paths that are present in a particular environment you select or are assigned and draw arrows that might suggest the meaning of the path graphically. Notice how this exercise relates more closely to Exercise 2d.

b. Identify various nodes in the environment and draw graphic symbols for each. Remember that each is relative to context.

c. Develop a list of districts and graphic representation for each. Notice the relationship between paths and nodes, and districts.

d. Identify examples of edges and develop graphic symbols for each. Once again notice the relationship between paths and nodes, and districts and edges.

ENVIRONMENTAL PRINCIPLES

In addition to design principles, there are also environmental principles that need to be considered when you develop design ideas. These principles, like the environmental elements, should support the basic design fundamentals and strengthen the design-graphics relationships.

Again, keep in mind that design and environmental images are interdependent and build upon each other. You should begin, if you have not already, to visualize these relationships and evaluate your design ideas more comprehensively. When completing the exercises, consider not only information discussed in the immediate example, but also the information discussed throughout this book. You should be synthesizing this information as part of your mental design process development.

Relationships

In an environment there are numerous relationships that exist between various elements and ideas. Understanding and developing these relationships is a key to successful design. In a previous description of relationships defined by paths, the example of the attraction of a children's play area to an elementary school was presented. Simple relationships as well as more complex ones, require a great deal of thought and decision making. This book, however, does not delve into mental approaches to problem solving. It discusses only a few aspects of relationships that you as a designer will undoubtedly encounter as you proceed in your design-graphics interests.

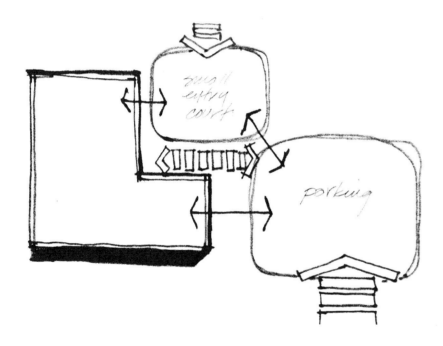

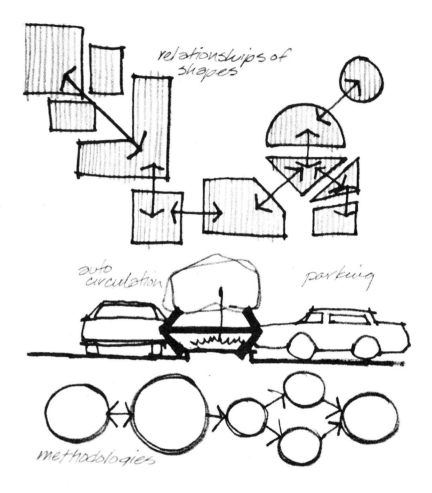

Form and Function Relationships. The term "form" is used here to describe all of the relationships that have been discussed relative to the elements and principles of design. It suggests the aesthetic relationships that should be present in a successful design idea. Functional relationships, on the other hand, are relative to the working mechanisms of a successful design, such as roads and automobile circulation, or a sense of privacy and screening fences. Most design problems will require synthesis and evaluation of a full range of both these relationships.

Form Follows Function. A very popular phrase in design that suggests an interdependent relationship between the two fundamental relationships of a form and function is that "form follows function." This implies that form is subordinate to function, but it should nevertheless be thought of as a supportive relationship. Each relationship builds off the other, and neither should be disregarded in developing the overall design solution. As you develop your understanding of design and the design process, you will undoubtedly develop your own ideas about this relationship and its application to your work.

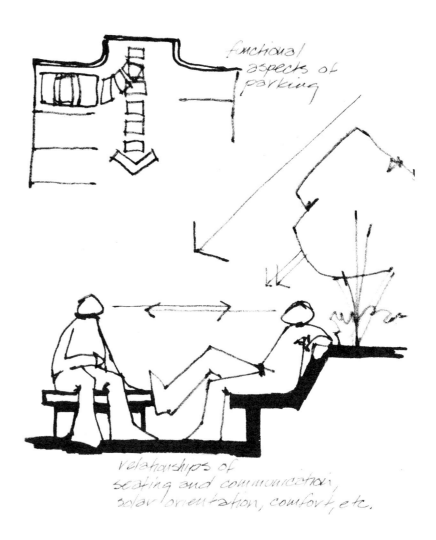

functional aspects of parking

relationships of seating and communication, solar orientation, comfort, etc.

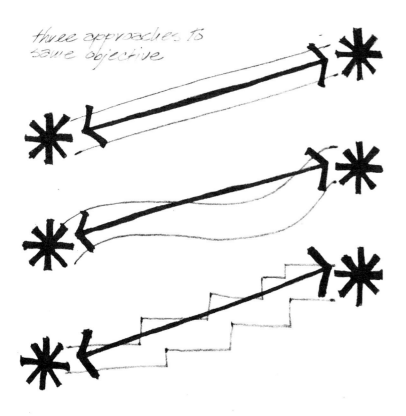

three approaches to same objective

Exercise 10: RELATIONSHIPS

a.   Use the graphic examples of environmental elements provided earlier in this chapter to create an abstract image for the following relationships: street-yard-house-fence, street-playground-school-sidewalk, highway-city-state-university, scenic lookout-trail-forest-waterfall and others of your choice.

b.   Produce a relationship diagram for an organization, or event, such as a family, faculty, curriculum, or project flowchart.

c.   Identify various examples of "form follows function" in the environment.

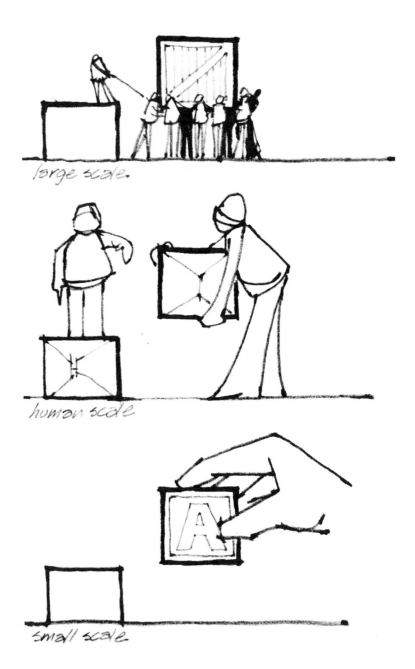

large scale.

human scale

small scale.

Scale

When one describes various relationships in the environment, one often refers to their size or their "scale." Scale is an important principle that establishes a frame of reference. In design-graphics, there are two basic scale references that are essential to consider—human and measured.

Human Scale. Each individual's basic frame of reference in the environment is him/herself. An adult may perceive the environment as being massive, comfortable, or miniature, depending on the scale of the elements. Evaluate the following examples of human scale and notice how details of the elements are also related to scale. Generally speaking, the more detailed the elements, the smaller the scale.

Measured Scale. As you refine your design ideas, you will probably need a means for describing scale relationships more accurately. In this instance you may wish to utilize measured scales. These scales are made by assigning a desired length to a given unit. For example, if something is "one quarter scale," it is understood to be one-fourth its actual size.

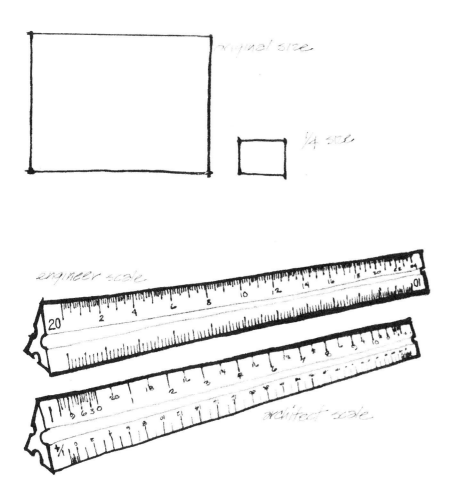

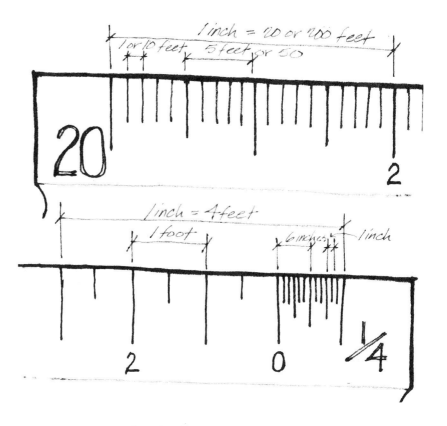

Instruments that facilitate conversions of length are called "scales." The architect scale assigns measurements of feet and inches to various increments of the inch. For example ¼ inch may represent 1 foot, (written ¼" = 1'0") and is divided into 12 equal units representing inches. In the same manner, the engineer scale assigns increments of 10 feet to the inch. For example, 1" = 20'0" indicates that the inch is divided into 20 equal units, each representing one foot. By multiplying or dividing the number by 10 you can increase or decrease the assigned length. For example, 20'0" × 10 = 200'0", means that 1 inch equals 200 feet with individual units representing 10 feet.

Proportion

Proportion is an important principle directly related to scale. It is the relationship of vertical and horizontal measurement. As you analyze the environment, you become more aware of various relationships between these two proportions. For example, the human body is divided into proportionate parts, the head being approximately one-eighth of the entire body length, and the arm span approximating human height. Knowledge of these and other proportionate relationships can help you evaluate the environment more readily.

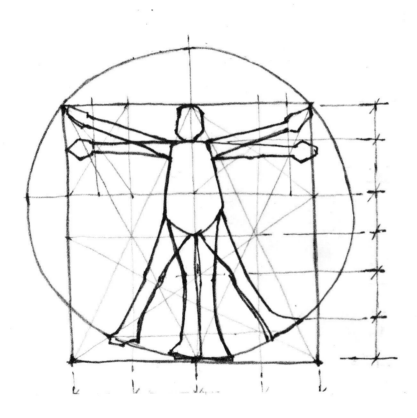

When elements in the environment are "out of proportion," there is a lack of harmony between horizontal and vertical aspects of the design. Understanding proportion and applying it to the design-graphics process can also help you to develop ideas rapidly and effectively without the use of measured scales.

Exercise 11: SCALE and PROPORTION

a. Trace the scale figure (a), then, using the scale figure as a reference, complete the drawing adding the other elements. Place your work over the original to evaluate your accuracy.

b. Using photographs, replicate the instructions used in Exercise 11a to produce a proportionate image. Remember to evaluate the directionality of the lines and shapes, in addition to their size.

c. Identify the lengths of the given lines as indicated by the assigned measured scale.

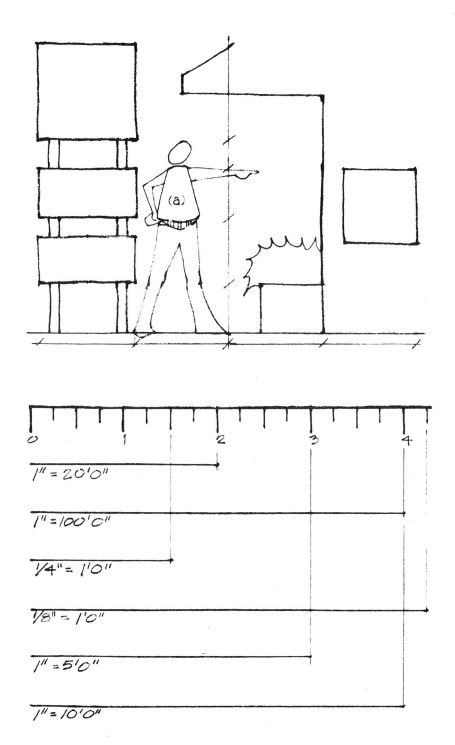

Photo by Theodore D. Walker

$1'' = 20'0''$

$1'' = 100'0''$

$1/4'' = 1'0''$

$1/8'' = 1'0''$

$1'' = 5'0''$

$1'' = 10'0''$

51

Photos by Theodore D. Walker

3

Graphic Images

As you develop your design-graphics ideas for your own evaluation, or for the evaluation of others, you will want to utilize a variety of "graphic images." These images will help you explain different aspects or characteristics in your design. Many of these images have been used throughout the book, and their application to design may already be well understood. It is important to remember the names of these images, as they, unlike many of the names in this book, are universal in their meaning.

Another important thing to remember is that these images are still only conceptual in nature and don't require detail or refinement. Quick and effective utilization of these images is far more important than illustrative rendering. For this reason, no exact measurements, or drafting technique will be used in explaining these terms.

ORTHOGRAPHIC PROJECTIONS

An orthographic projection is a two-dimensional image of the environment, with no foreshortening or distortion of measurement. Such images are very useful for fundamental communication of design ideas.

The **plan** shows a view looking down on the environment, where only descriptions of horizontal relationships are discernible.

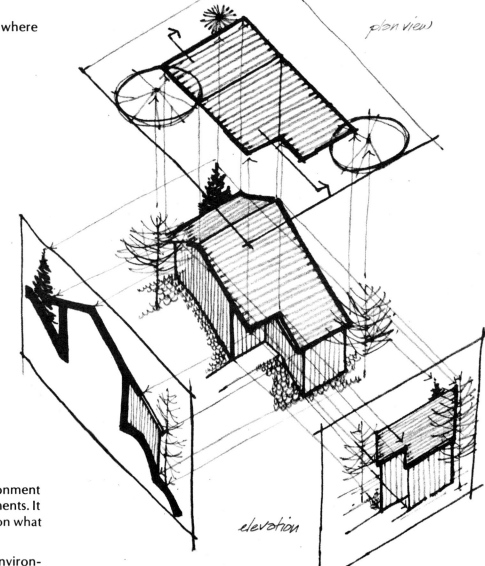

plan view

section

elevation

The **section** is a very useful image that describes the environment as if it were sliced through, exposing a view of its structural elements. It can be used as either a plan view or an elevation depending on what information in the section is important to communicate.

The **elevation** is a view looking perpendicular to the environment from any angle describing relationships of verticals and horizontals.

54

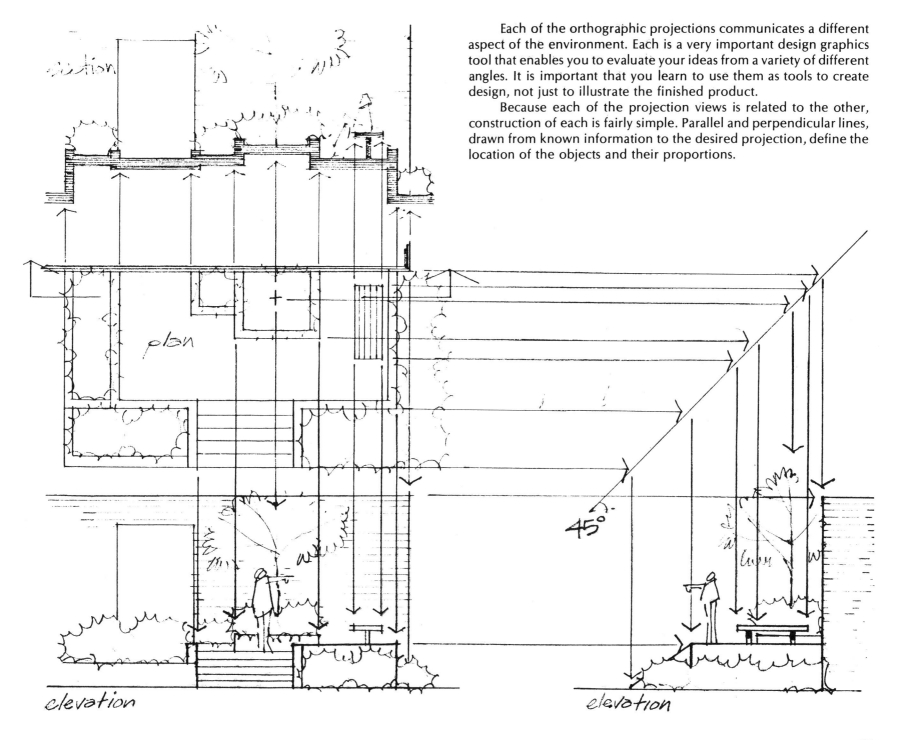

section

plan

45°

elevation

elevation

Each of the orthographic projections communicates a different aspect of the environment. Each is a very important design graphics tool that enables you to evaluate your ideas from a variety of different angles. It is important that you learn to use them as tools to create design, not just to illustrate the finished product.

Because each of the projection views is related to the other, construction of each is fairly simple. Parallel and perpendicular lines, drawn from known information to the desired projection, define the location of the objects and their proportions.

Exercise 12: ORTHOGRAPHIC PROJECTIONS

a. Produce a plan view image from the two elevations given to the right. Remember that a 45° angle will aid in the conversion.

b. Produce the three remaining elevation images for the plan given on the next page.

c. Produce two sections from the plan and elevation information. Arrows on the section line indicate the direction of the observer's view.

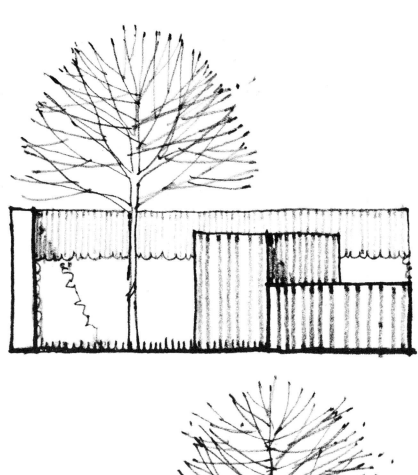

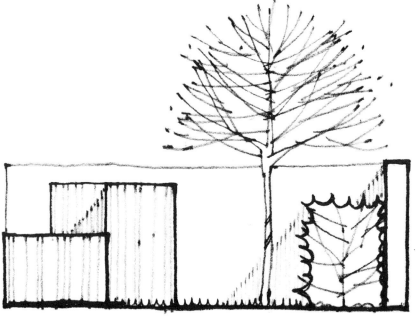

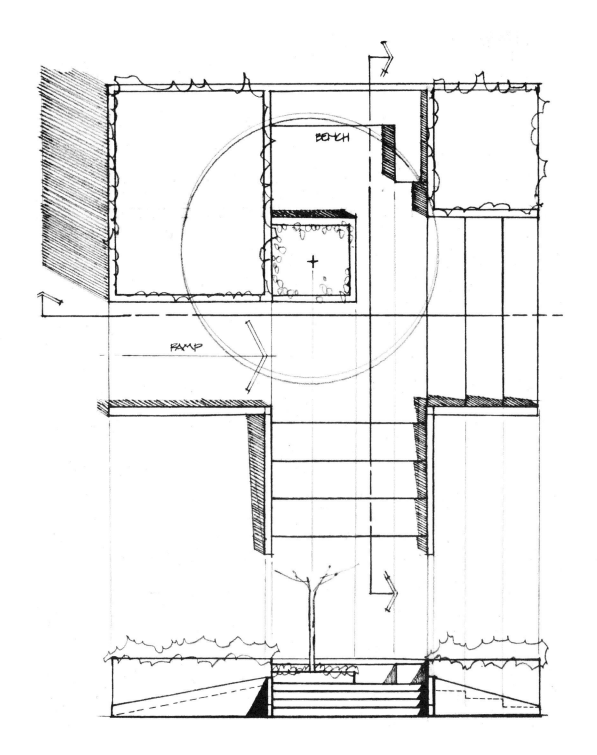

BENCH

RAMP

PARALINE

Paraline images have already been used in defining and portraying three-dimensional form (see isometric form Chapter 1). As the name suggests, lines that are parallel in reality are drawn parallel in this type of image, with little or no foreshortening or distortion of measurements. There are typically two types of paraline images that you should become familiar with in order to develop your ideas three-dimensionally.

Most of the spatial elements portrayed thus far have been *isometric* paraline images. The isometric is created by distorting the perpendicular angles of the elements, while maintaining accurate measurements for the parallel lines. What results is a three-dimensional image with distorted diagonals. It is extensively used because it is a rapid graphic technique and spatial description. Most isometrics are constructed using a 30° × 30° angle to create the base. However, a variety of combinations of angles may be used. Measurements are made along known edges, and vertical lines are drawn vertically and also measured accurately. Study the examples of isometric paraline images, and notice how the view changes relative to the angles used; the more the angle approaches 90°, the higher the apparent vantage point. The more the angle approaches 180°, the more the vantage point seems to relate to human scale.

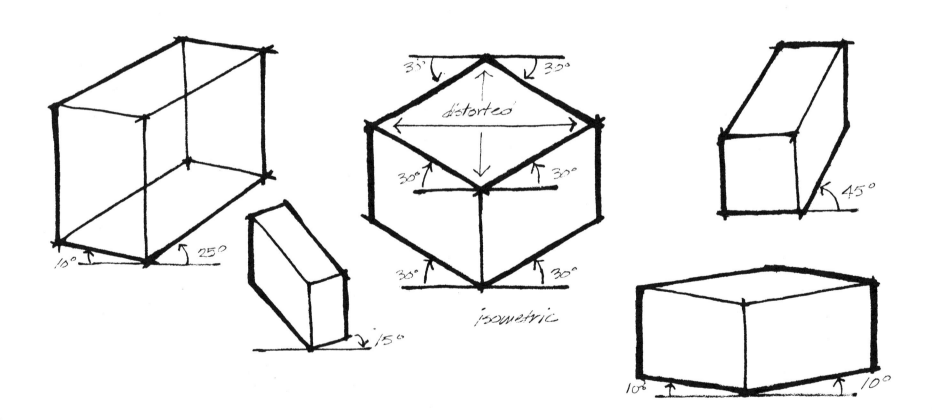

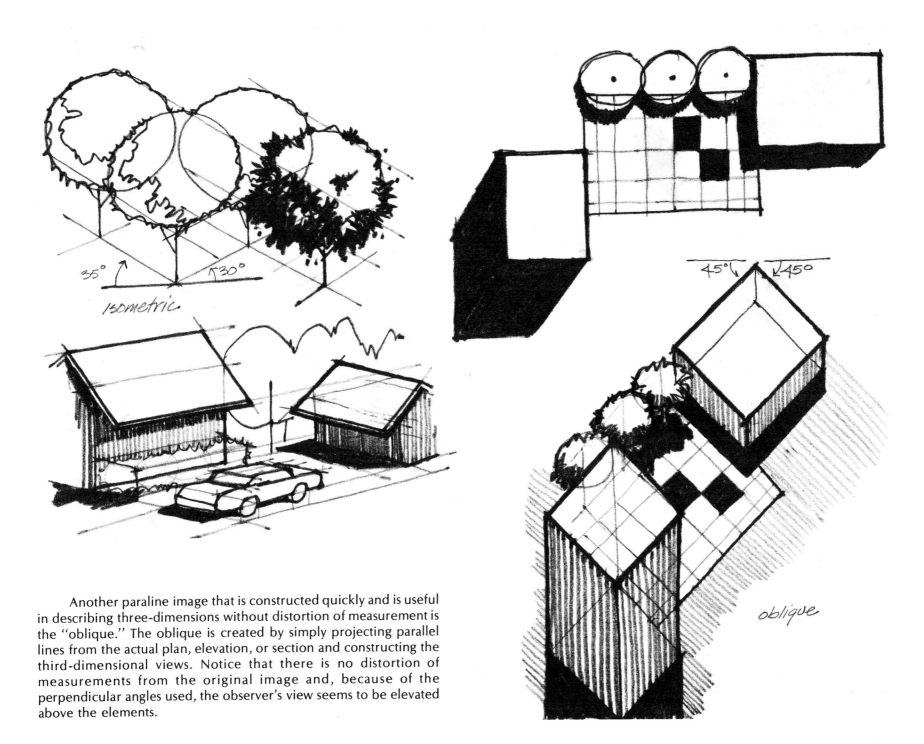

35° 30°

Isometric

45° 45°

oblique

Another paraline image that is constructed quickly and is useful in describing three-dimensions without distortion of measurement is the "oblique." The oblique is created by simply projecting parallel lines from the actual plan, elevation, or section and constructing the third-dimensional views. Notice that there is no distortion of measurements from the original image and, because of the perpendicular angles used, the observer's view seems to be elevated above the elements.

Exercise 13: PARALINE

a. Produce an isometric (30° × 30°) image from the plan and elevation information which follows. Remember that all lines are parallel to the 30° lines or the vertical lines.

b. Produce an oblique (45° × 45°) image from the same plan and elevation information.

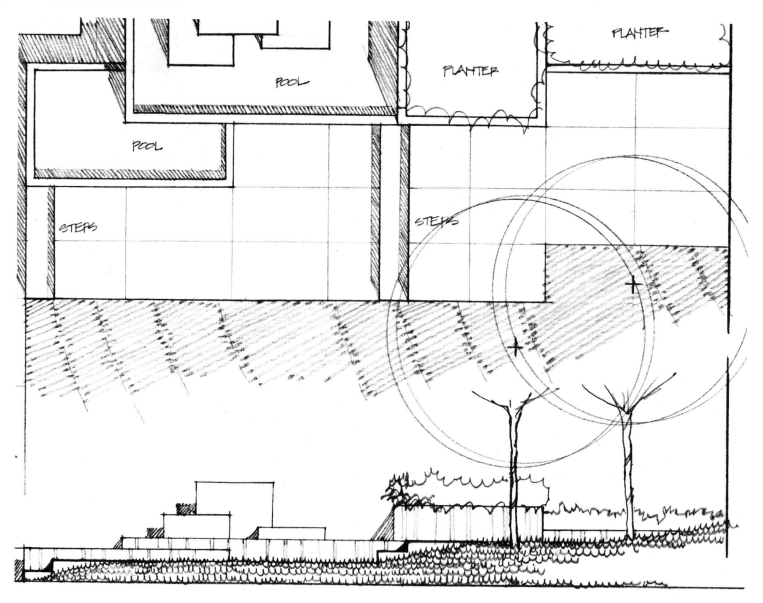

PERSPECTIVE

Perspective is perhaps the most useful of all the graphic images, because it describes the environment as it appears to the observer. In order to develop perspective images, you should be aware of a few important aspects of perspective.

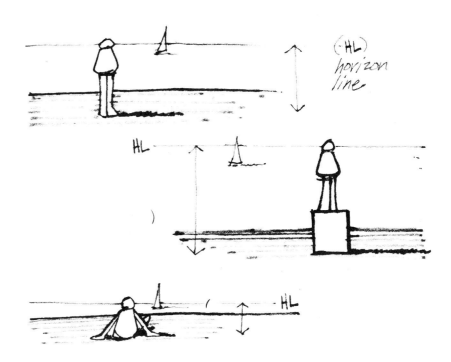

The *Horizon Line* is typically described as the line created by the earth meeting the sky. It is the level of the observer's line of sight above and parallel to the ground plane. As the observer's line of sight moves higher, the horizon line moves higher and more ground plane is visible. The reverse is also true.

The *Station Point* is the relative position of the observer to the environment which determines the angle of the line of sight. a 60° cone of vision is a helpful reference for locating the position of the station point in the plan view.

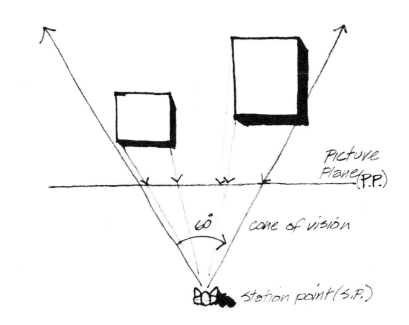

The *Picture Plane* is the two-dimensional transparent plane through which the observer sees the environment. Points that are perceived in perspective are recorded on the picture plane at the exact location where they pierce it relative to the line of sight. For most common methods of constructing perspective images, the picture plane is used for actual scale measurements.

61

Vanishing Points are points in the perspective image where common parallel lines meet. All lines in the environment have a vanishing point. Their locations are relative to the direction of the line itself and the observer's line of sight.

VP for roof lines

Vanishing points

HL

equal heights on level plane have same horizon line, no matter the position on ground

HL

GL

The *diminution property* of perspective causes the actual size of elements to appear smaller as they move further away from the observer. This is a fundamental principle of our perception of the environment and very important to the perspective image.

The *ground plane* is the two-dimensional plane relative to the earth's surface. It is composed of a multitude of *ground lines* that suggest different locations along the plane.

Construction of the perspective image can be accomplished in a variety of ways, both technical and approximate. For purposes of rapid communication of ideas at the conceptual design-graphics level, consider the latter. You should become familiar with the other, however, as you progress to more detailed refinements of your design ideas.

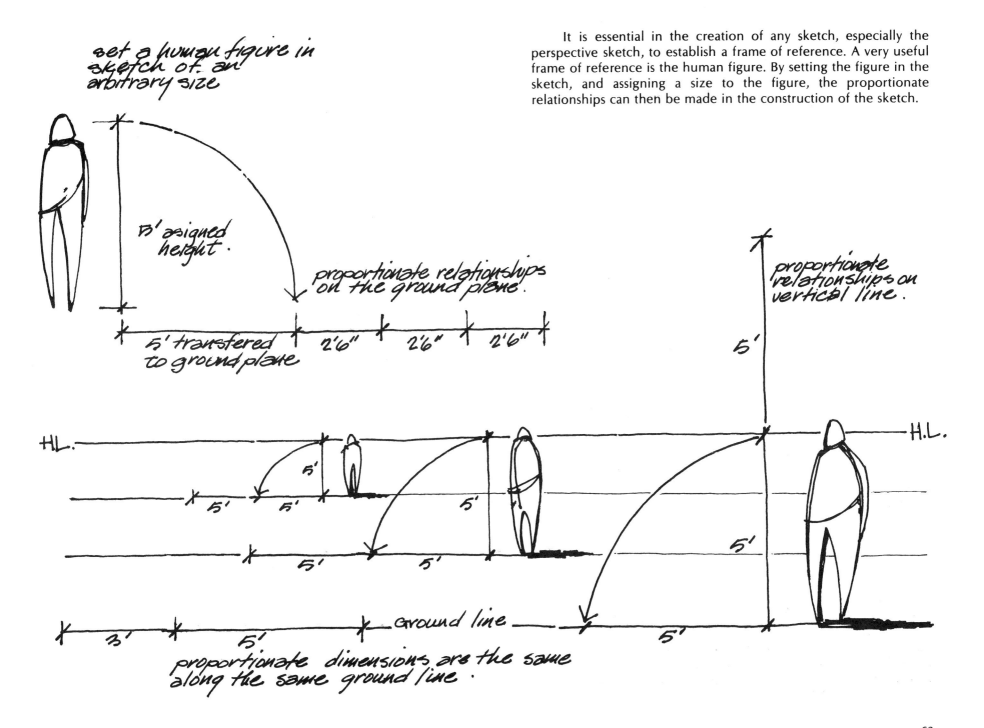

set a human figure in sketch of an arbitrary size

It is essential in the creation of any sketch, especially the perspective sketch, to establish a frame of reference. A very useful frame of reference is the human figure. By setting the figure in the sketch, and assigning a size to the figure, the proportionate relationships can then be made in the construction of the sketch.

5' assigned height.

proportionate relationships on the ground plane.

5' transfered to ground plane

2'6"   2'6"   2'6"

proportionate relationships on vertical line.

5'

HL.

5'   5'

5'

5'

5'   5'

5'

H.L.

3'   5'

ground line

5'

proportionate dimensions are the same along the same ground line.

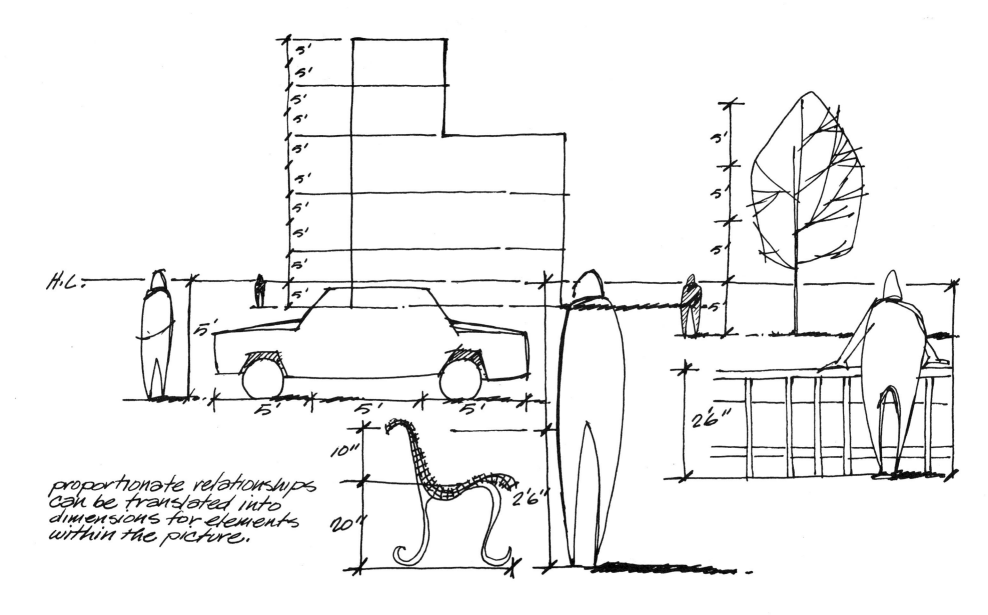

H.L.

5'
5'
5'
5'
5'
5'
5'
5'
5'
5'
5'

3'
5'
5'

5'

5'   5'   5'

2'6"

10"
20"
2'6"

proportionate relationships
can be translated into
dimensions for elements
within the picture.

The figure will establish a point on the ground plane and the
horizon line that can be translated into important perspective
concepts. This means that any figure placed on the ground plane, with
the same horizon line will have similar proportionate relationships
along the ground plane at that point. These relationships can then be
expanded into developing proportions and sizes of elements that
occur in the sketch.

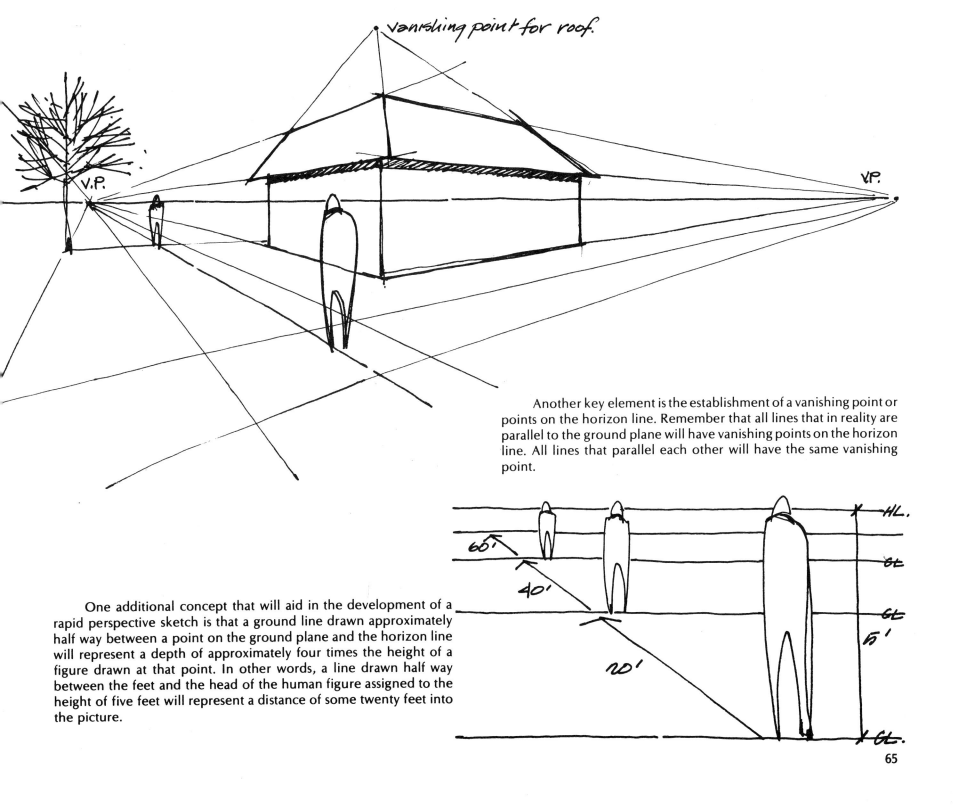

vanishing point for roof.

V.P.

V.P.

Another key element is the establishment of a vanishing point or points on the horizon line. Remember that all lines that in reality are parallel to the ground plane will have vanishing points on the horizon line. All lines that parallel each other will have the same vanishing point.

One additional concept that will aid in the development of a rapid perspective sketch is that a ground line drawn approximately half way between a point on the ground plane and the horizon line will represent a depth of approximately four times the height of a figure drawn at that point. In other words, a line drawn half way between the feet and the head of the human figure assigned to the height of five feet will represent a distance of some twenty feet into the picture.

HL.

GL

GL

5'

60'

40'

20'

GL.

65

By combining these simple concepts of perspective, one can rapidly develop a perspective sketch for preliminary design studies, or refine the sketch for more definitive communication needs.

The following examples demonstrate the use of proportion in developing rapid perspective sketches for preliminary studies. Notice that in some of these examples, the use of a section line has been incorporated to assist in the development of proportional relationships.

Multi-Use Area at Forest Street

MGA Land Planners

67

68

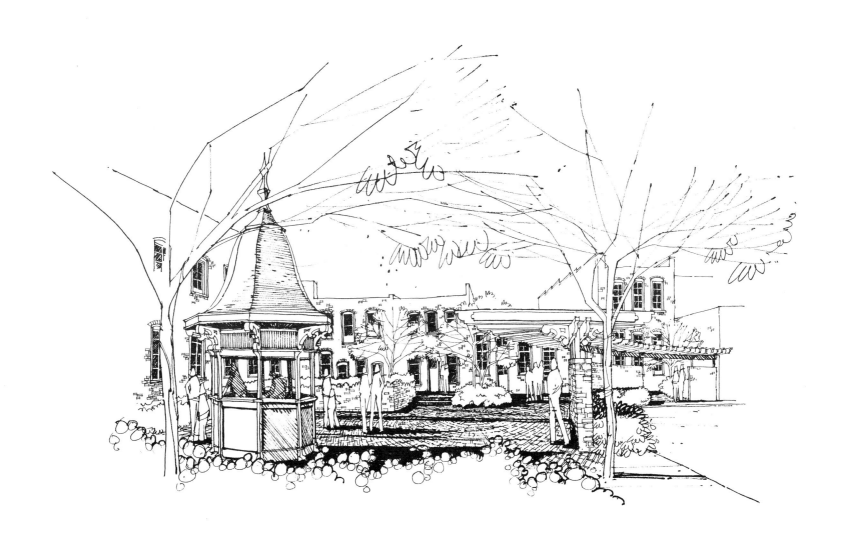

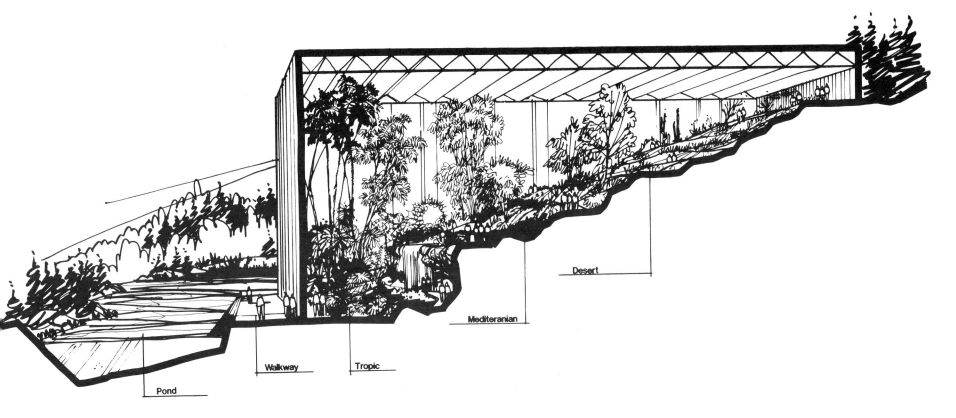

Pond

Walkway

Tropic

Mediteranian

Desert

Conservatory

MGA
Land Planners and Landscape Architects

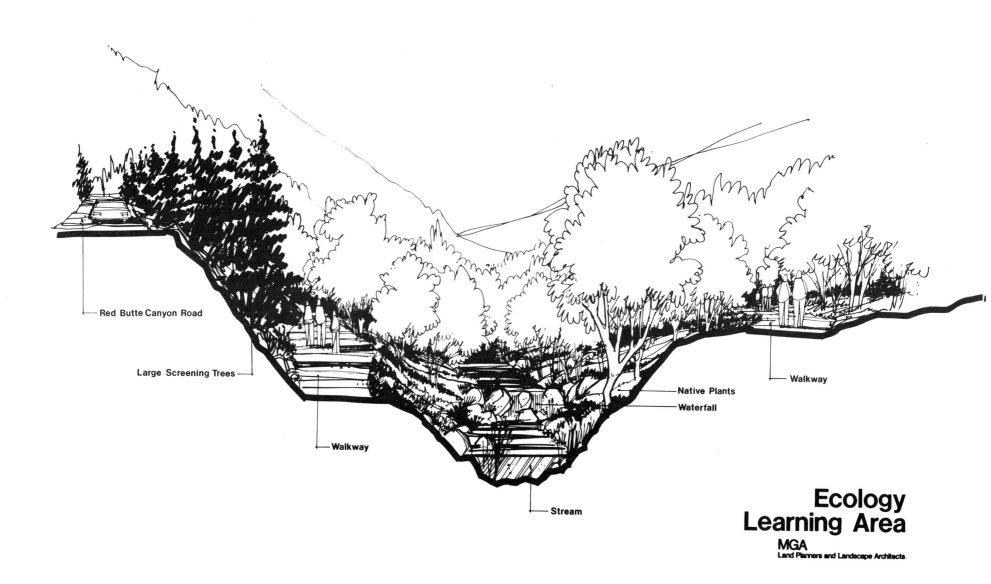

Red Butte Canyon Road

Large Screening Trees

Walkway

Stream

Native Plants

Waterfall

Walkway

**Ecology
Learning Area**
MGA
Land Planners and Landscape Architects

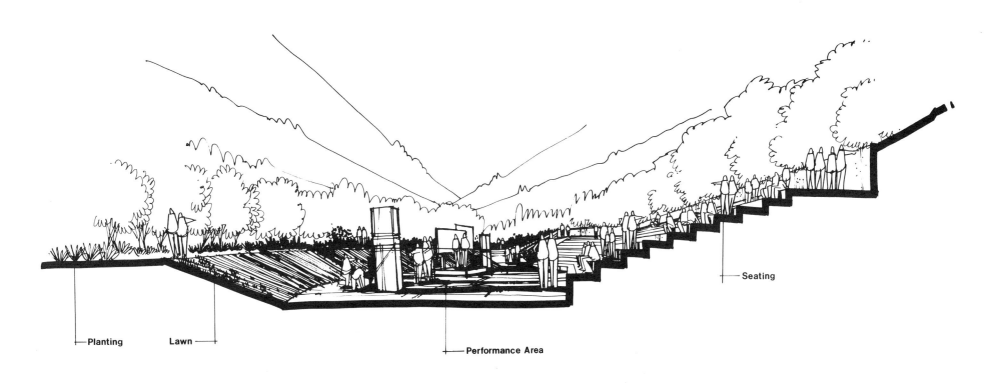

├─Planting   Lawn─┤

├─Performance Area

├─Seating

Amphitheater
MGA
Land Planners and Landscape Architects

73

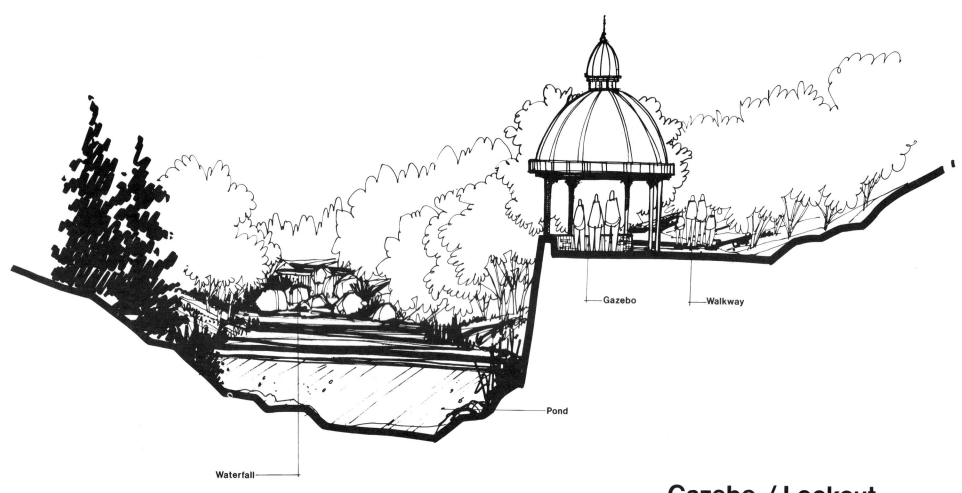

Gazebo

Walkway

Pond

Waterfall

Gazebo / Lookout

MGA
Land Planners and Landscape Architects

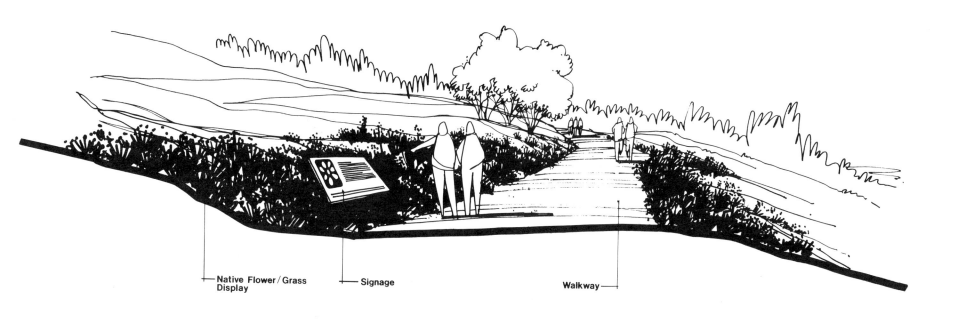

├─ Native Flower / Grass   ├─ Signage   ├─ Walkway ─┤
      Display

Interpretive Trail System
MGA
Land Planners and Landscape Architects

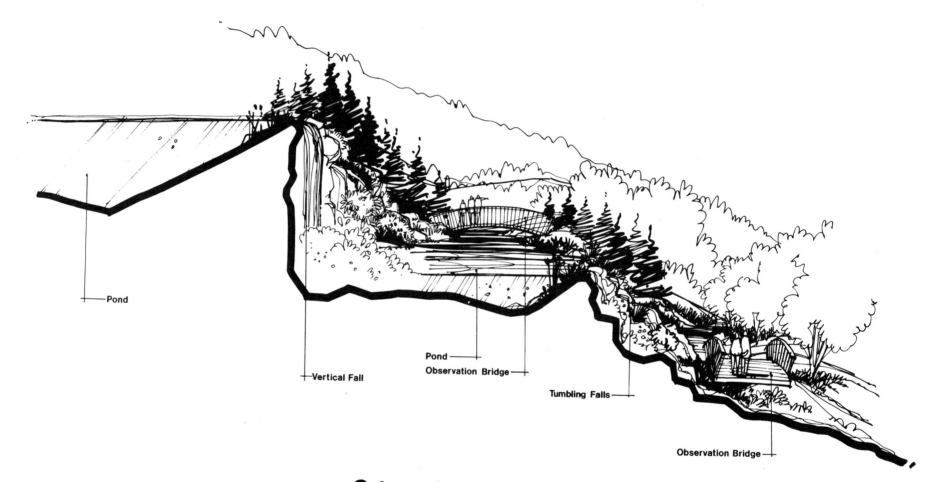

Pond

Vertical Fall

Pond

Observation Bridge

Tumbling Falls

Observation Bridge

Oriental Display / Waterfall Features
MGA
Land Planners and Landscape Architects

76

One Point Perspective Grid. The one point perspective suggests that the observer is standing perpendicular to the environmental element and that lines parallel with the sight line vanish to one point on the horizon line. Lines that are perpendicular to the observer are drawn as horizontal lines, and vertical elements are drawn with vertical lines.

For most beginning design students, it is easiest to create perspective images using a grid system. This enables more accurate estimates of proportion more quickly.

Simple construction of the grid is based on proportionate relationships between the ground plane and the horizon line. Diminution is created by establishing a vanishing point for 45° diagonals that intersect the grid lines creating perspective squares.

Study the following examples and notice that for each perspective image the grid is the same, only the proportions differ. For this reason, you should save your accurate perspective grid.

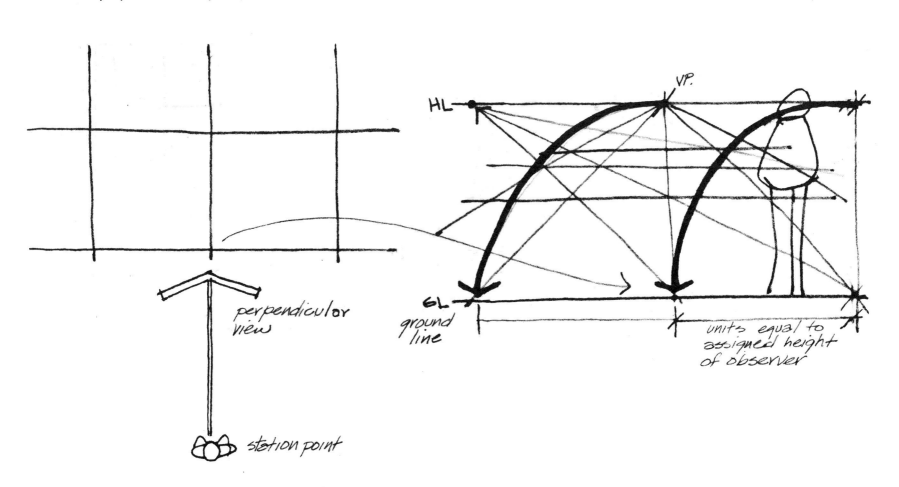

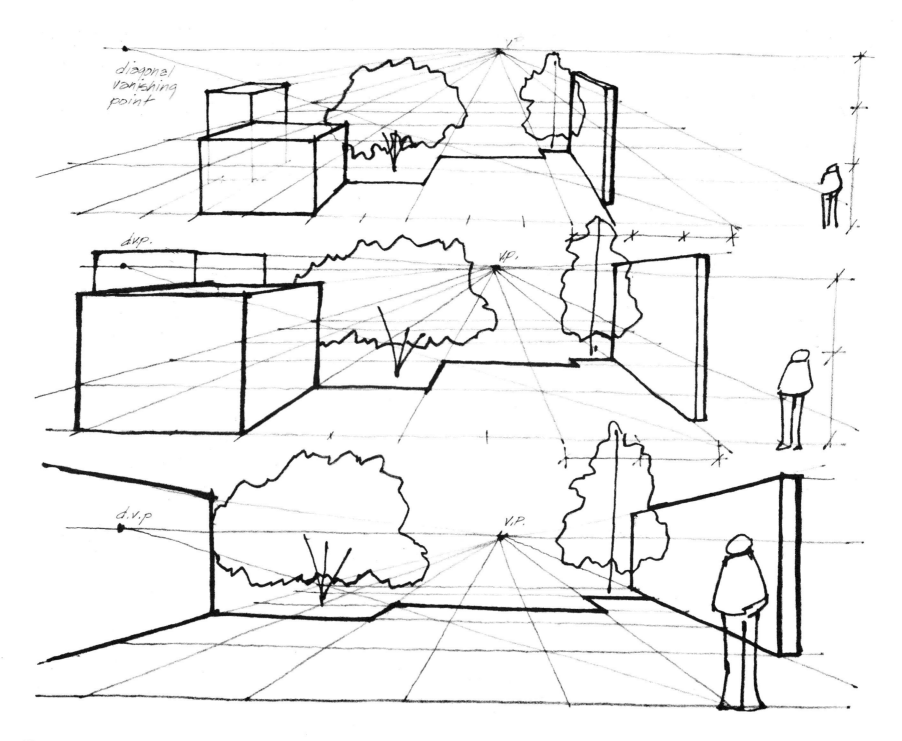

diagonal
vanishing
point

d.v.p.

v.p.

d.v.p.

v.p.

d.v.p

v.p.

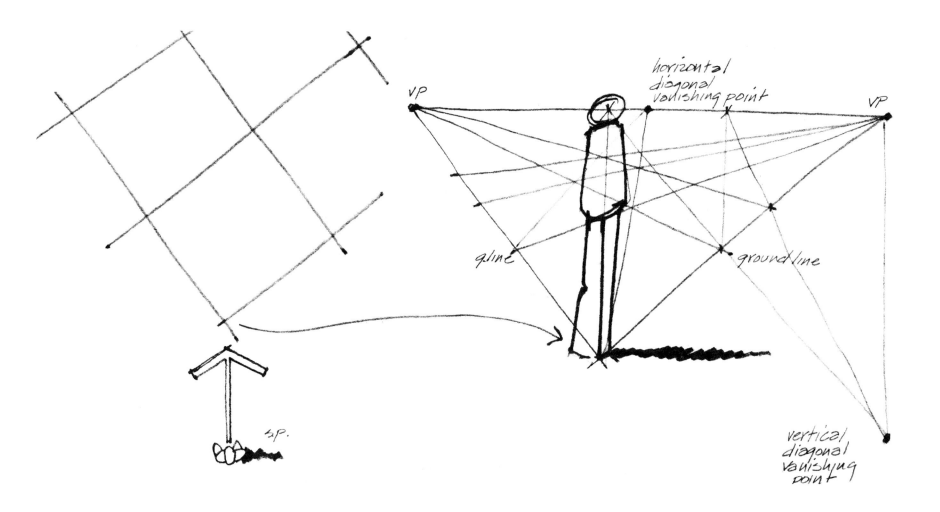

horizontal diagonal vanishing point

VP

VP

q line

ground line

vertical diagonal vanishing point

s.p.

Two Point Perspective Grid. Two point perspectives suggest that the observer's line of sight is something other than perpendicular to the environmental elements. This creates a perspective grid with two vanishing points on the horizon line for all parallel lines.

Diminution is once again based on locating 45° diagonals that intersect and create squares in perspective. Notice that direct proportionate relationships between the lines on the ground plane and the horizon lines are no longer possible. All proportionate estimates have got to relate to the principle of diminution.

Study the examples of the two point perspective and again notice that the proportions change, but the grids remain the same. Once you have a few perspective grids accurately constructed, you can make numerous perspective images of design ideas as they might appear three-dimensionally.

79

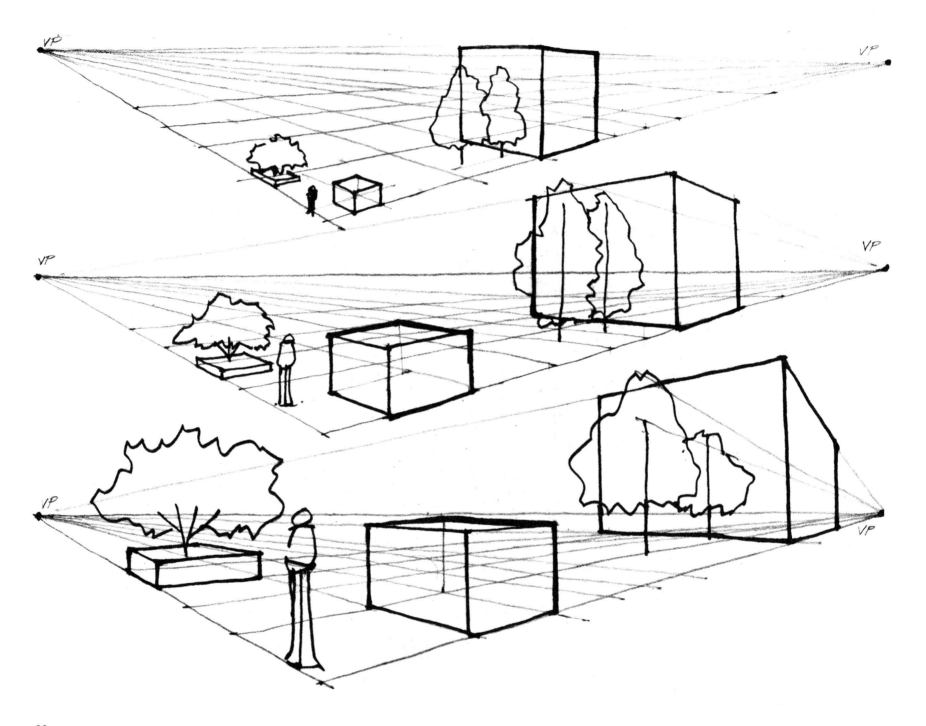

Exercise 14: PERSPECTIVE

a. Produce a one point perspective image from the plan and elevation given on the next page. Remember that all parallel lines vanish.

b. Produce a two point perspective image from the same plan and elevation.

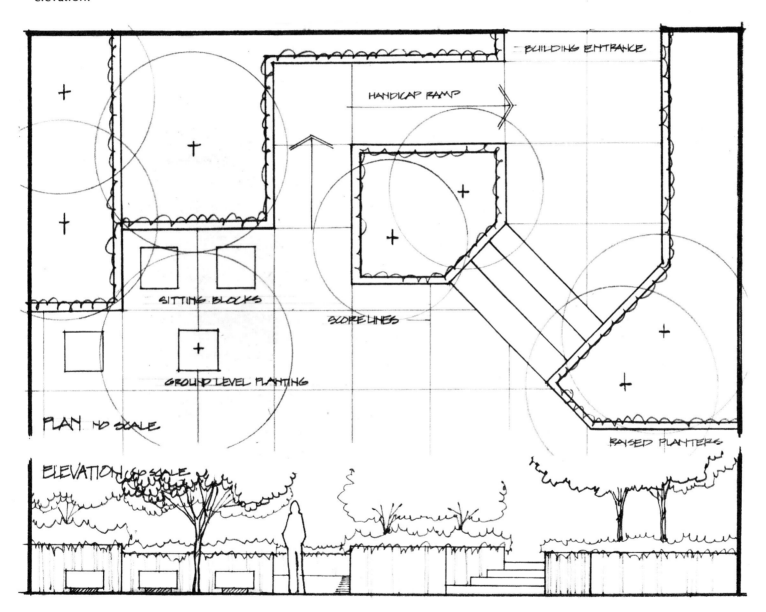

BUILDING ENTRANCE

HANDICAP RAMP

SITTING BLOCKS

SCORE LINES

GROUND LEVEL PLANTING

PLAN NO SCALE

RAISED PLANTERS

ELEVATION NO SCALE

4
Design Process

The introductory section of this book defined the design progressive process of evaluation, synthesis, and refinement of design ideas. To illustrate how the design process actually works, the following chapter presents a hypothetical design problem and solution.

Suppose that you were asked to design an outdoor area for a small townhouse apartment. You would undoubtedly need to inventory the elements of the problem area and then evaluate them in terms of their potentials and constraints. This is often referred to as the site analysis. The evaluation however, should include not only the physical site analysis, but also other variables that relate to the design solution, such as the needs of the townhouse residents, maintenance, legal regulations, neighbors, etc.

All of this information then needs to be collected or synthesized in order to create possible design alternatives. Synthesis of this information represents the creative design "battlefield" mentioned earlier. This is where potentials and constraints are pitted against each other to develop reasonable approaches to resolving the problem.

Once you have developed several alternative approaches to design, you will need to refine those alternatives in order to select those that resolve the problem most effectively. The more you refine your ideas, however, the more you will need to synthesize your information and evaluate your results, thus the cycle continues.

DESIGN PHASES

Because the design process does not have a set beginning or end—just a recycling of information and ideas, it is difficult to try to describe the design process step by step. There are, however, a number of design phases which help to structure the process, and which usually occur in a sequential pattern. You will remember these phases from the introductory diagram: analysis, program, schematic and design development.

Again, remember that the initial phases are related to conceptual design-graphics, and the communication of ideas among interested designers. Graphics at this level of design development are thinking graphics. Illustrations and rendered detailings are needed only to the extent that they enhance that thinking process. Concern for details, whithout proper evaluation, synthesis and refinement of basic design and environmental principles, may result in energy exhausted on a poor design solution.

Analysis Phase

The analysis of a design problem is important in determining conditions and characteristics of the situation that may influence the final design solution. As in the townhouse example, an analysis should be an evaluation of the existing potentials and constraints relative to the design problem. The analysis may include information about the physical characteristics of the site, such as geology, geography, climatology, spatial configurations, etc. It may include information about human or wildlife characteristics that are related to the site, such as relationships between individuals and groups, physical and psychological needs, etc. It may even include legal and economic information, such as zoning and building ordinances, or capital and investment financing.

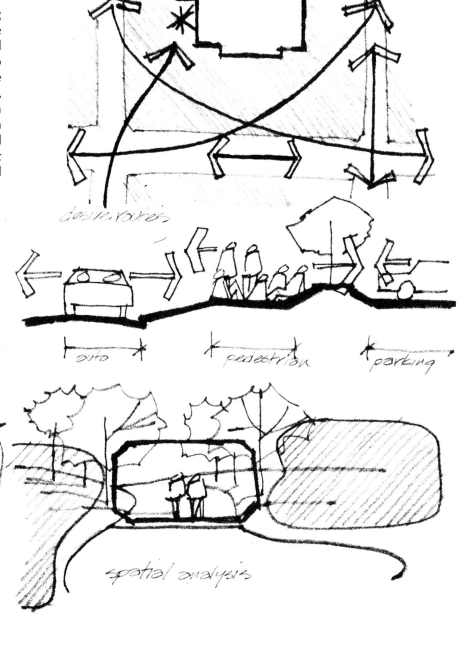

desire routes

auto   pedestrian   parking

spatial analysis

visual / spatial

Program Phase

A very important phase involves defining the goals and objectives of a design proposal. Often called collectively the "program," it gives meaning and direction to the design process and serves as a yardstick for measuring the progress and development of the design ideas.

During the first stages of design, the program may be very general in its definitions. However, as the design advances, and more information is available, it is helpful to also refine and develop the program itself. This way you will have more specific parameters about which to structure your design solution.

The development of the program, like the entire design process, may require some "give and take" decision making. For this reason, you should learn to utilize design-graphics in your decision making processes in order to visualize potential design outcomes. Learn to think with graphics!

Schematic Phase

The schematic phase is difficult to pinpoint relative to its place in the design sequence. Most likely it begins as soon as the design problem is conceived. It refers to that phase of design where potential approaches and solutions begin to take shape, mentally and graphically. It describes the initial development of design alternatives, often called schematics, or concepts.

Whatever the name used, it represents an important part of design. Schematics are frequently stressed as the foundation upon which the design solution is constructed. Therefore, you should develop your schematics based on good analyses, programs, and fundamental design principles.

Design Development Phase

Refinement of your schematics and development of probable design alternatives is the next phase of design. As with the other phases, the development phase will require decision making and creative intuition in order to refine those ideas with the most promise of success.

Graphically the design becomes increasingly more detailed with regard to form and functional relationships. Design and environmental elements evolve from abstraction to realism. In this refinement phase, basic shapes and forms in concept now become plant materials, structures, roads, etc.

The design development phase is just one step behind the finalization of the design solution. It implies the designer is ready to present the ideas for the review of other interested persons, such as the client or public. It does not, however, mean that it is the end of the design process. A lot of work has yet to be done before the design becomes reality.

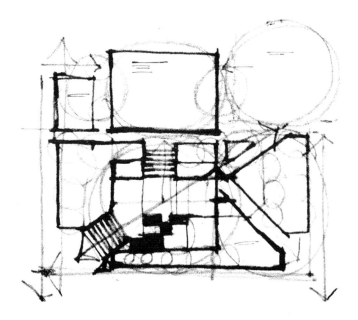

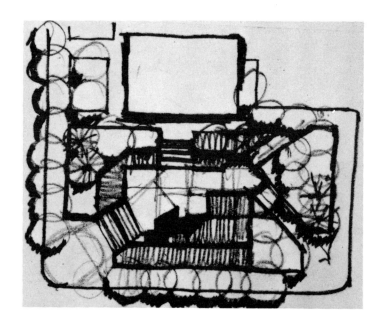

DESIGN SUGGESTIONS

Students, just beginning in the design curriculum and even those who may have been with it for awhile, often feel frustrated and discouraged by their inability to produce effective design solutions quickly. Anyone who has been involved in design can sympathize with those feelings. As a follow-up to this chapter on the design process, here are a few ideas that may help ease these frustrations and speed up the design process.

■ Develop a hands-on rapport with the design-graphics relationships. Use graphics to help you visualize your ideas as you conceive them. Develop the link between your mind and your pencil, and practice, practice, practice.

■ Learn to utilize the graphic technique that fits the occasion. If you are just beginning a design, in the schematic phase for example, "quick and dirty" graphics are all that is necessary. Put aside your T-square, triangles, or templates, and get a soft pencil that makes quick, bold strokes. Your ideas are still rough, and your graphics should also be rough. That is why you should develop a freehand graphic ability so as not to rely on mechanical drawing instruments that may inhibit free-flow ideas.

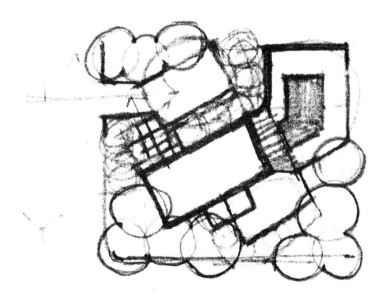

■ Develop complete ideas. Don't stifle your progress in design by evaluating every line and relationship as you proceed. Quickly portray an idea, and then evaluate it comprehensively. From one idea you can then develop complete alternative ideas.

■ Console yourself with the realization that there are few instances of perfect design. There are many students who "bottom out" at the schematic phase of design trying to develop the ultimate design solution. There are different approaches to design and different solutions for the same design; one being no more perfect than the other. Once you have some feasible concepts, develop them. Select the one that you decide best resolves the problem, and "run with it."

■ Use the suggestions of others to *enhance*, not demolish, conceptual design ideas. Designers, instructors, and even other students are helpful in the design process because they have their own ideas about a problem, but so do you. If your conceptual foundation is sturdy, don't destroy it and erect another based on outside ideas, simply apply their suggestions as they relate to that concept.

■ Organize yourself and work quickly. No one will ever know how much time you spend on a design project. Often students complain that they spent a lot of time on a particular problem but still received a bad grade. Your effort is not an indicator of your design quality. For this reason alone, you need to develop design ideas quickly and resolve problems rapidly. You also need to organize your efforts so you don't spend time repeating your work. Don't dive into a problem without a little foresight as to where you are headed.

■ Develop your design by building from conceptual and schematic design ideas. Students will frequently develop a bubble diagram of relationships for a design, set it aside, and then begin to work out a final design solution. This is like plotting a cross-country trip and then forgetting to bring the map. Develop a system of laying tracing paper over your concepts and building solutions from them. This way you will always relate to, and build upon solid design ideas. Your design solution will virtually evolve from conception to completion in this manner.

■ Work conscientiously at developing your understanding of the environment and the design principles that create it. This is the best way to become a good designer.

from conception to completion

REFERENCES

The following is a list of recommended books that support the information presented in the previous section.

Arnheim, R., 1969. *Visual Thinking*. Berkeley, CA: University of California Press. 345 pages.

Ashihara, Y., 1970. *Exterior Design in Architecture*. New York: Van Nostrand Reinhold. 143 pages.

Faruque, O., 1984. *Graphic Communication as a Design Tool*. New York: Van Nostrand Reinhold. 320 pages.

Gibson, J., 1950. *The Perception of the Visual World*. Boston, MA: Houghton-Mifflin. 235 pages.

Gill, R.W., 1980. *Basic Perspective*. London: Thames and Hudson, Ltd.

Hanks, K., Belliston, L., 1980. *Rapid Viz: A New Method for the Rapid Visualization of Ideas*. Los Altos, CA: William Kaufmann, Inc. 157 pages.

Hanks, K., Belliston, L., 1977. *Draw? A Visual Approach to Thinking, Learning and Communicating*. Los Altos, CA: William Kaufmann, Inc. 242 pages.

Hartmann, R., 1976. *Graphics for Designers*. Ames, Iowa: Iowa State University Press. 124 pages.

Laseau, P., 1980. *Graphic Thinking for Architects and Designers*. New York: Van Nostrand Reinhold. 212 pages.

Lockhard, W.K., 1982. *Design Drawing*. Tucson, AZ: Pepper Pub. 267 pages.

Lockhard, W.K., 1977. *Drawing as a Means to Architecture*. Tucson, AZ: Pepper Pub. 112 pages.

Lynch, K., 1960. *The Image of the City*. Cambridge, MA: MIT Press. 194 pages.

McHarg, I., 1971. *Design with Nature*. Garden City, NY: Doubleday Natural History Press. 197 pages.

McKim, R., 1980. *Experiences in Visual Thinking*. Monterey, CA: Brooks-Cole Pub.

Samuels, M., Samuels, N., 1975. *Seeing With the Minds Eye*. New York: Random House.

Sausmareg, M., 1983. *Basic Design: The Dynamics of Visual Form*. New York: Van Nostrand Reinhold.

Scott, R.G., 1951. *Design Fundamentals*. New York: McGraw-Hill. 199 pages.

Simonds, J.O., 1983. *Landscape Architecture*. 2nd Edition. New York: McGraw-Hill. 331 pages.

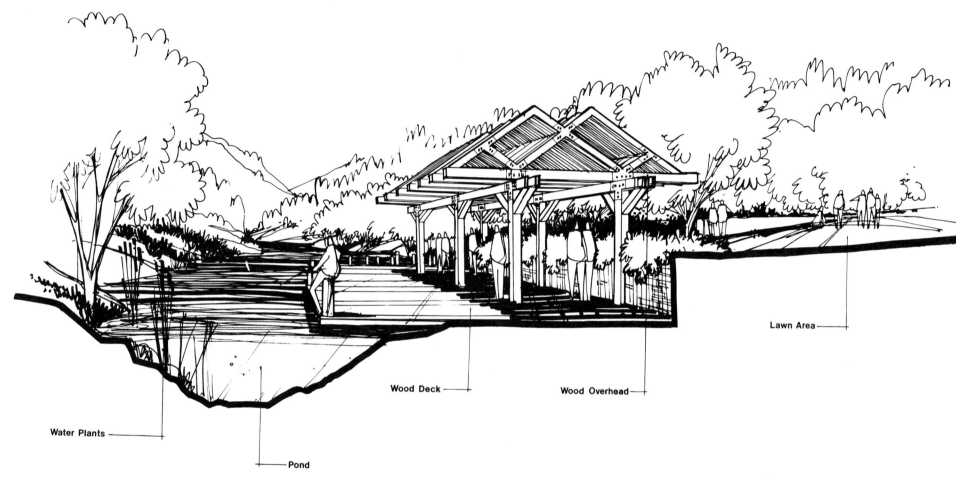

Water Plants

Pond

Wood Deck

Wood Overhead

Lawn Area

Homescape

SECTION B

REPRESENTATIVE DESIGN-GRAPHICS

This section describes the more refined aspects of the design-graphics process. It relates to a different group of users and, therefore, a different level of graphic communication. Representative design-graphics are used to present conceptual and proposed design solutions to those persons who may not have been directly involved in the design process.

This level of design-graphics does not, however, mean that the design process is finalized. In reality a design idea is not finalized until it is built or put into effect. Therefore, remember that although the design idea is more detailed than at the conceptual design stage it is still subject to further evaluation, synthesis, and refinement. This also means that quick, yet effective, communication of ideas is essential. The discussion and exercises in this section will suggest various design-graphics approaches to communicating design ideas in a representative or presentation form.

5

Visual
Communication I

Two basic forms of visual communication are the written word, and the graphic image. This chapter concentrates primarily on the latter, but it is important for you as an environmental designer to develop your abilities in both.

The development of visual communication skills, like the development of the design process, also involves a process of evaluation, synthesis and refinement of information. As you examine the material in this book, as well as any other examples of visual communication, you should ask yourself several questions: What is important? How is it accomplished? How could it be improved?

There are no set rules for communicating ideas graphically. Each designer may have a different approach for any number of similar graphic images. Consider, however, a few key principles that may help you to develop visual communication-graphic skills.

LINE

In graphic communication, as in other design-graphics areas, the line is fundamental. It not only serves to delineate design ideas, but when used properly, it can also give life or realism to the graphic images. Three aspects of line that help to produce this effect are control, quality, and variation.

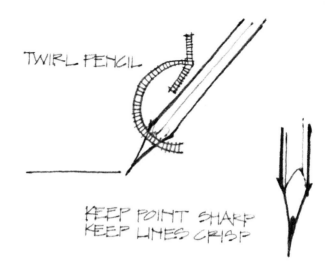

TWIRL PENCIL

KEEP POINT SHARP
KEEP LINES CRISP

Line control has been defined as the conscientious effort to communicate line with meaning and intention. Hopefully you are beginning to develop a sense for good line control and understand its importance in visual communication and design idea refinement.

Line quality implies that the line is consistent in its width and density. Twirling the pencil slightly while delineating is an effective approach to good, crisp line quality. Because much of representative design-graphics involves reproducing information, good line quality is essential to good reproduction.

SECTION LINE

BOUNDARY-PROPERTY   HEAVY

OBJECT LINE

HIDDEN LINE   MEDIUM

PROPOSED CONTOURS

EXISTING CONTOURS

SCORE LINES   THIN

DIMENSION - EXTENSION

GUIDELINES   FINE

Line variation or line weight variation is a very important aspect of effective and meaningful visual communication. By varying the width of a line for example, you can give variety to a graphic image, while maintaining unity. Line variation can produce areas of emphasis, detail, and perceptions of depth. It can also be used to describe different types of line. Study the following examples and notice that the quality and control of the line are constant, only the line weights vary.

LETTERING

Because the written word is also used to communicate design ideas, it is essential that graphic representation of those words be effective. Collectively, written information is referred to as lettering. Lettering, like line, should be controlled, varied when necessary, and display good line quality for reproduction. Other characteristics of effective lettering include consistency, balance, uniformity, and overall legibility. Using guidelines, and keeping your lettering style fairly simple will help to produce these characteristics.

Beginning design students may want to model their lettering style from examples of others before developing a lettering style of their own. The following examples of upper and lower case lettering are styles quite often used among environmental designers. environmental designers.

Frequently an effective way to evaluate a person's fundamental graphic ability is to examine their freehand lettering. You should become proficient at freehand lettering, not only for rapid communication of written information, but also for development of overall delineation abilities.

ABCDEFGHIJKLMNOPQRSTUVWXY
1234567891011213

ABCDEFGHIJKLMNOPQRSTUV

ABCDEFGHIJKLMNOPQRSTUVW

abcdefghijklmnopqrstuvwxyz
ABCDEFGHIJKLMNOPQRSTUVWXY
1234567891011 12
abcdefghijklmnopqrstuvwxyz

ABCDEFGHIJKLMNOPQRST

ABCDEFGHI
JKLMNOPQ
RSTUVWXYZ

BASIC LETTERING CONSTRUCTION

A HELPFUL APPROACH TO UNIFORM LETTERING IS TO USE A T-SQUARE AND TRIANGLE FOR ALL VERTICAL LINES.

Exercise 15: LINE and LETTERING

a. Redraw the example to the right applying the appropriate line weights as indicated.

b. Using the guidelines provided below, practice your lettering: the alphabet; upper and lower case, numbers, and writings of your own choice.

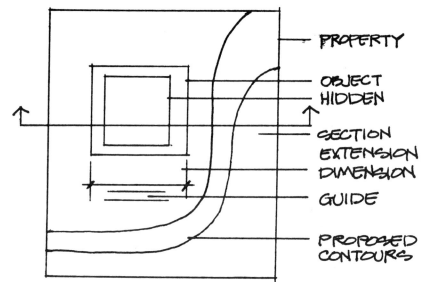

PROPERTY

OBJECT

HIDDEN

SECTION

EXTENSION

DIMENSION

GUIDE

PROPOSED
CONTOURS

LOOK

The overall look or appearance of representative design ideas is a very important principle of visual communications. Whether the information is graphic or written, it should be portrayed in a meaningful and competent manner. Good characteristics of line and lettering are fundamental to this principle. Other characteristics include format and composition.

Presentation of design ideas often requires careful and thoughtful preplanning to insure that the ideas are communicated effectively. Many times students with good design ideas, are unable to organize them for presentation purposes. As a result, the design process is difficult to comprehend and the potentiality of the presented ideas is often disregarded or discredited.

First impressions of design ideas, like first impressions of people, have a powerful impact and are often based entirely on outward appearance. For this reason you should continually develop your representative design-graphics skills, as well as other communication skills, in order to produce a professional first impression. Although you may not as yet be of professional status you never will be unless you strive for it.

Format

The term "format" refers to the unified look of information as it relates to the entire representative design idea. For example, this book has a certain sheet format: 8½" × 11" page, horizontal orientation, headings, 4¼" columns, print type, spacing, margins, etc; all unified as a whole.

The format for presentation material helps hold together the various aspects and ideas of the presentation information.

There is no standard format for presentation information. Each design may prescribe a different format in order to communicate specific information. There are, however, several pieces of information that are normally included, especially when graphic images are being represented. These include scale (graphic and/or written), north arrow, title of project, description of graphic image (analysis, for example), and date.

Title blocks and borderlines are other aspects of format that are commonly used in developing format styles. A rule of thumb that might be used is the width, or "strength," of the borderline and titleblock is relative to the sheet size. The pages of this book, for instance, would not lend themselves to ½ inch border lines, and a two inch titleblock.

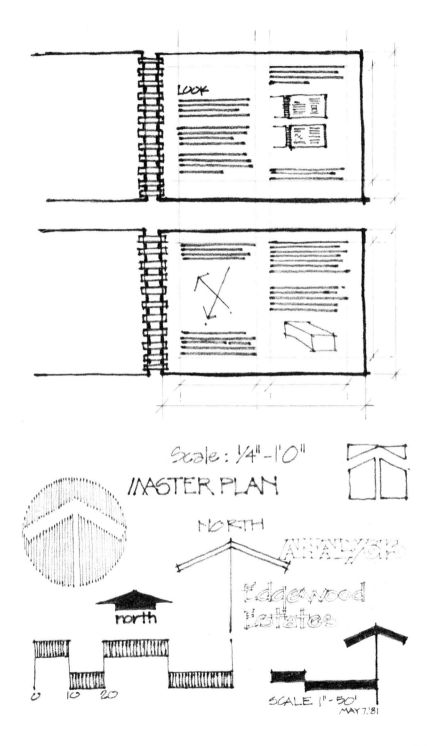

Composition

The composition, or organization of presentation information, is very important to the professional appearance and communication of design ideas. The various pieces of graphic and written information need to be carefully considered and arranged in order to produce a compositionally sound presentation. Often this organization requires some preplanning and careful evaluation.

Composing presentation material often becomes a design problem in and of itself. In this regard, it might be helpful to evaluate your material in terms of the design principles that were discussed earlier. Is there unity, balance, and emphasis among the various written descriptions and graphic images? Does the presentation information appear to "hang together"?

Purpose

This final principle is merely a summation of all the principles relative to visual communications. It is a reiteration of the fundamental principle behind graphic-communication in general; which is, graphic representation of design ideas should serve the purpose intended by the designer.

Visual communication is one part graphic skill and two parts mental evaluation. If you will strive to understand the fundamentals of visual communication techniques and then apply your understanding to develop your own graphic skills, you can improve your overall representative design-graphics abilities one hundred percent.

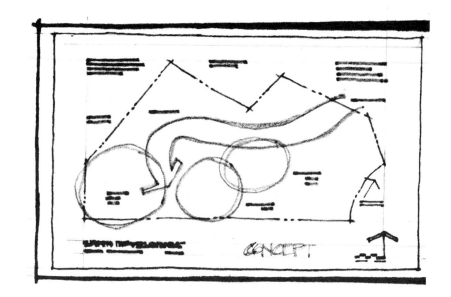

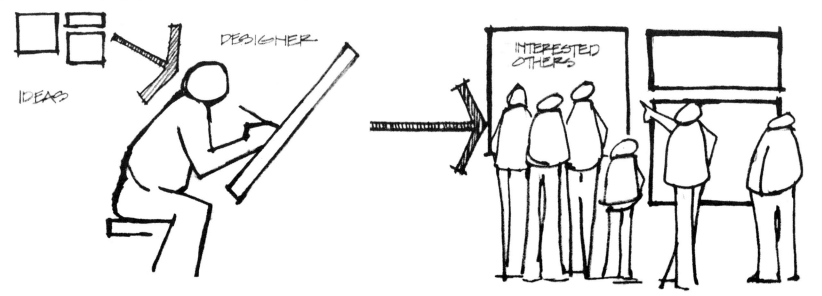

Historical

Leisure

Nature

Observation

Preservation

6
Visual Communication II

Visual communication of design ideas at a representative graphic level is a simple, but refined, description of the entire design process including analysis information, concepts or schematics, plans, elevations, sections, sketches, paraline or perspective drawings. Each one describing a different design phase, or design idea relative to the proposed design solution. In this chapter several graphic techniques that help represent these design ideas more effectively are identified.

Again you should remember that there are no standards for graphics or visual communication. The information discussed is suggested for application in a general sense. Therefore, consider this information generally, and then apply it toward developing your own visual communication ideas.

The principles of visual communications suggested in the preceding chapter provide the basis for the graphic techniques suggested in this chapter. It would be worth your while to have an understanding of these principles before proceeding in this book.

FUNDAMENTAL DESIGN PHASES

An important aspect of visual communication often overlooked is that of representing the fundamental phases of the design process, namely the analysis and schematic phases. Most students are saturated with information related to presenting developed design ideas, but representation of fundamental ideas is often neglected.

Much of the information presented in these phases is abstract, and not as easily portrayed as a tree or a building. This may in fact, be the reason why there is little mention of it in visual communication courses. Because these phases are the basis for more developed design ideas, however, they are equally as important to communicate as the advanced phases, and should be included in basic graphic instruction.

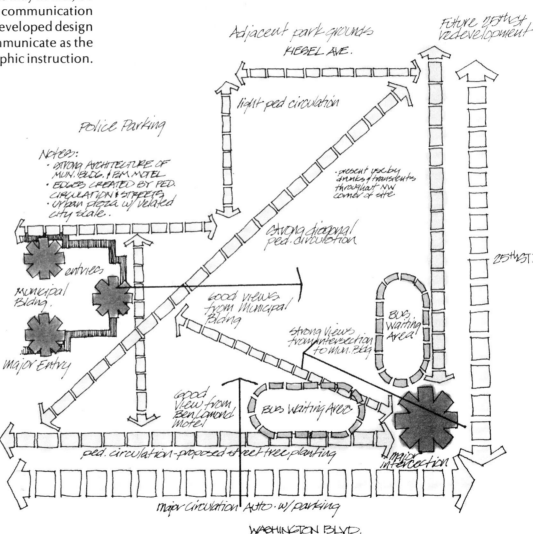

Analysis

The analysis phase often dictates the parameters about which the proposed design solution is founded; therefore, it should be included as part of the design solution presentation. This may be done in several ways. When extensive analysis is needed, the analysis information is often separated into various map forms for slope, vegetation, soils, etc. Other times it may be profitable to combine maps, such as slope and soil, to identify specific relationships. When less analysis is required, on a small site, for example, a comprehensive map of varied information may be all that is necessary to communicate the potentials and constraints of a design problem.

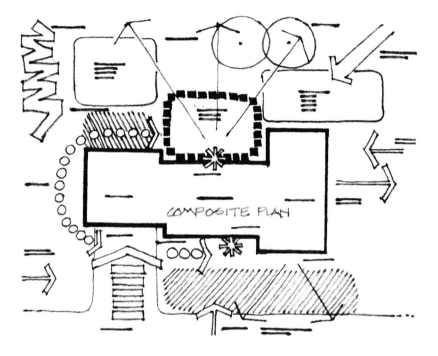

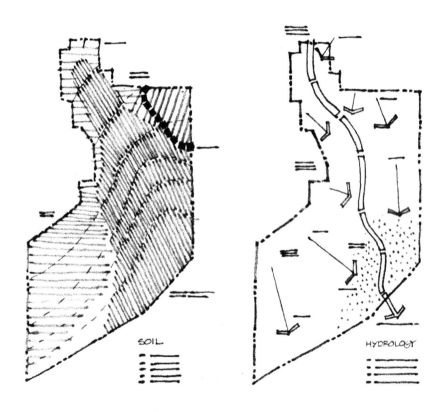

Much of the information must be communicated abstractly in the form of symbols and shapes. Visual communication of this information therefore, is best accomplished with bold, yet simple graphics. Other types of analysis information will need to be communicated in written form with notes or descriptions of the problem. Delineation, lettering, and organization of analysis information is therefore critical. Once again, evaluate what you want to communicate and how that communication can be accomplished.

The symbols and shapes used in presenting the analysis phase are based on the examples of environmental elements described in Chapter 2. A review of that chapter may help you understand the development of these techniques. Notice how the symbols and shapes have been refined at the representative design graphic level.

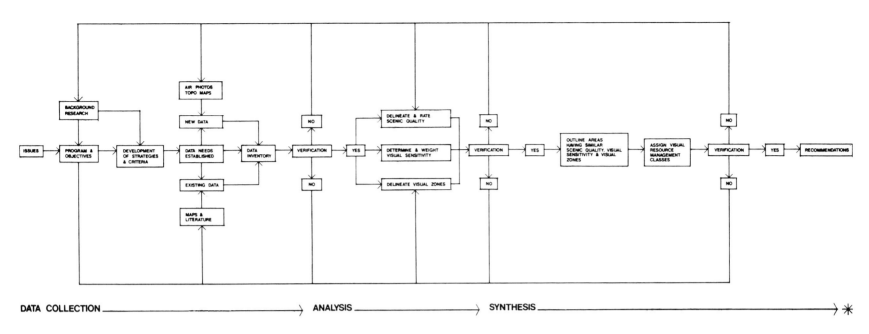

DATA COLLECTION ————————————→ ANALYSIS ————————→ SYNTHESIS ————————————————————→ ✳

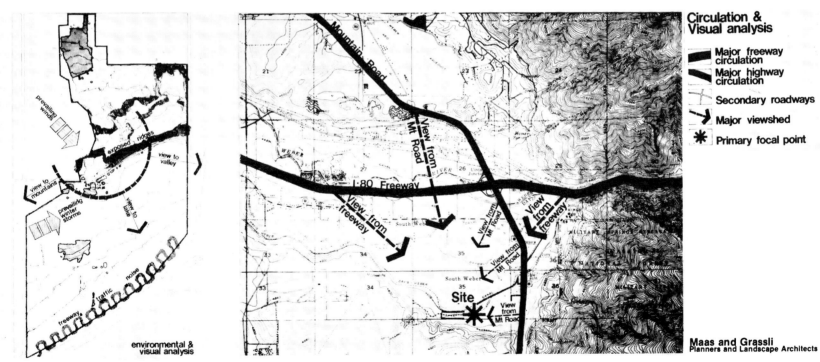

environmental &
visual analysis

Circulation &
Visual analysis

- Major freeway circulation
- Major highway circulation
- Secondary roadways
- Major viewshed
- ✳ Primary focal point

Maas and Grassli
Planners and Landscape Architects

101

Program-Concept

Other fundamental design phases that may need to be presented are the program and concept. These explain the goals and objectives and basic design ideas upon which the design solution is structured.

The concept requires bold and simple graphic symbols and shapes, with any needed supportive written information. Again, you must evaluate the purpose of the concept information, and then delineate, letter, and organize it so as to communicate the ideas most effectively. In many cases, the concept is descriptive of the proposed design solution even to the extent of having developed design characteristics, such as building shapes and vegetation. This is not a standard, however, and you should refine your concept information according to your own communication intentions.

Visual communication of the program and concept, like the analysis, is often abstract and requires simple graphic techniques that enable quick and effective understanding of design ideas. The program is usually an outline of the intended goals and objectives of the project. Perhaps the easiest way to develop the outline is to phrase it so as to complete the statement: "I propose to..." followed by a statement of the goals and objectives of the project. You will want to be sure to not only state the goals, but also indicate clearly how you intend to achieve those objectives.

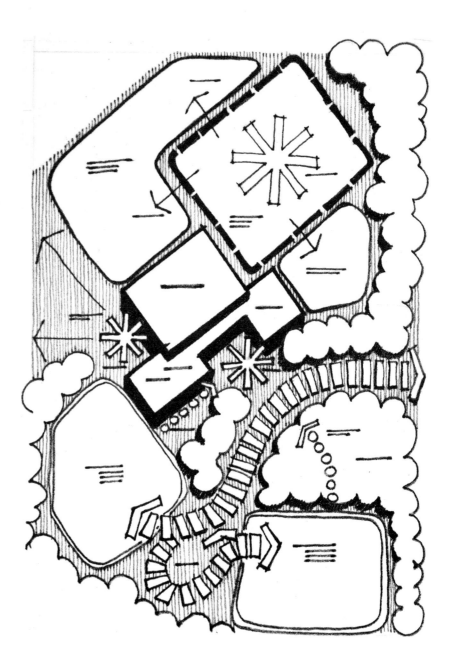

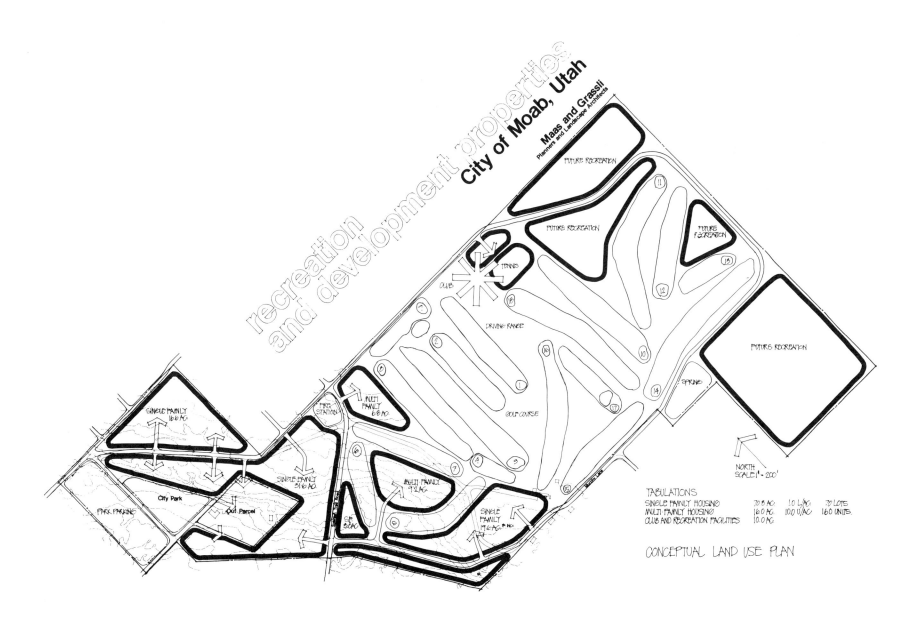

recreation
and development properties

City of Moab, Utah

Maas and Grassli
Planners and Landscape Architects

FUTURE RECREATION

FUTURE RECREATION

FUTURE RECREATION

TENNIS

CLUB

DRIVING RANGE

FUTURE RECREATION

SPRING

GOLF COURSE

SINGLE FAMILY
16.6 AC.

MULTI
FAMILY
6.8 AC.

FIRE
STATION

SINGLE FAMILY
31.6 AC.

MULTI FAMILY
9.2 AC.

City Park

Out Parcel

SINGLE
FAMILY
19.6 AC.

PARK PARKING

NORTH
SCALE 1" = 200'

TABULATIONS
SINGLE FAMILY HOUSING   70.8 AC.   1.0 L/AC.   70 LOTS
MULTI-FAMILY HOUSING   16.0 AC.   10.0 U/AC.   160 UNITS.
CLUB AND RECREATION FACILITIES 10.0 AC.

CONCEPTUAL LAND USE PLAN

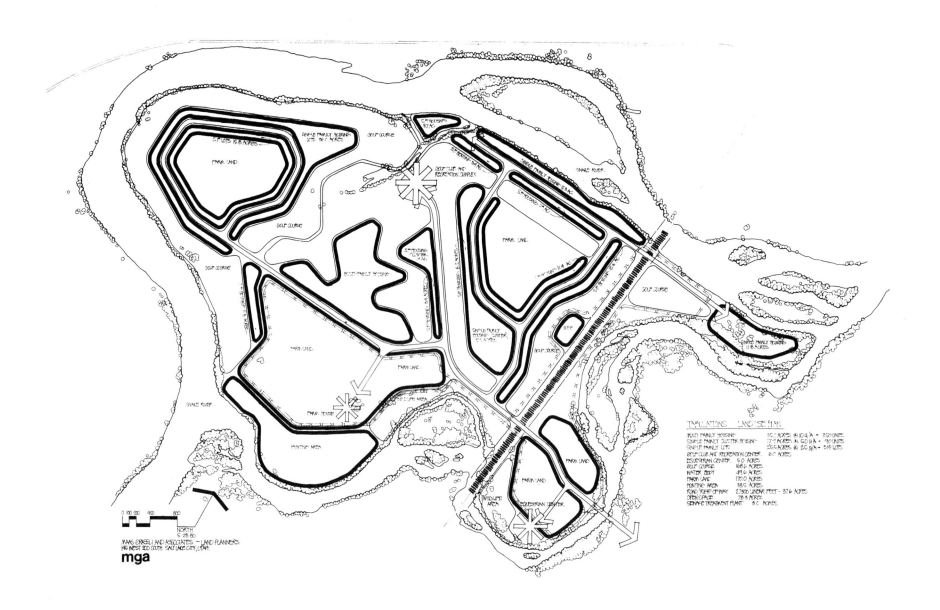

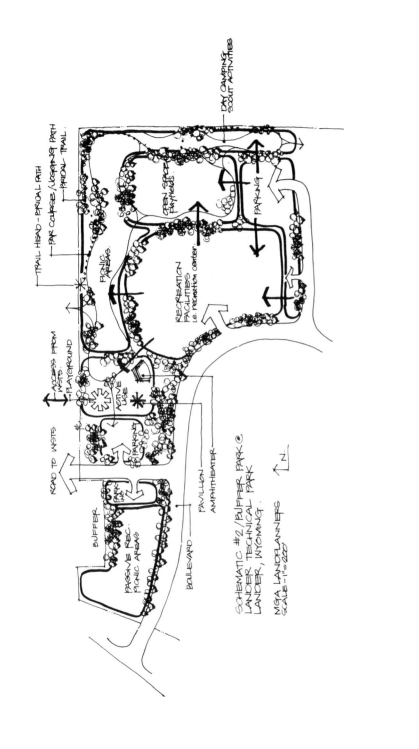

DAY CAMPING
SCOUT ACTIVITIES

TRAIL HEAD - BRIDAL PATH

PAR COURSE / JOGGING PATH

BRIDAL TRAIL.

OPEN SPACE
PLAYFIELDS

PARKING

PICNIC AREAS

RECREATION
FACILITIES
i.e. recreation center

ACCESS FROM
WSTS

PLAYGROUND

ACTIVE
USE

PARKING

ROAD TO WSTS

BUFFER

PASSIVE REC.
PICNIC AREAS

PAVILLION

AMPHITHEATER

BOULEVARD

SCHEMATIC #2 / BUFFER PARK @
LANDER TECHNICAL PARK
LANDER, WYOMING.

MGA LANDPLANNERS
SCALE - 1" = 200'

N.

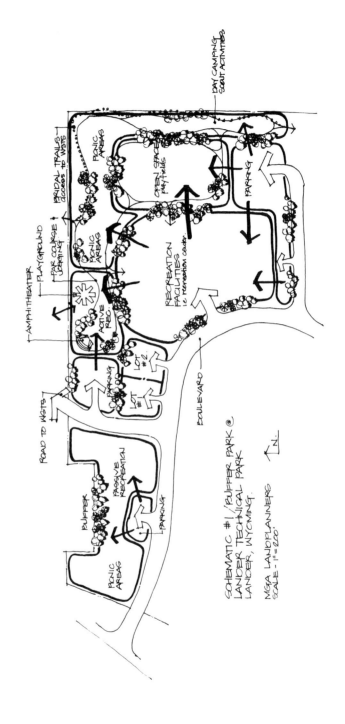

DAY CAMPING
SCOUT ACTIVITIES

PICNIC AREAS

OPEN SPACE
PLAYFIELDS

PARKING

PICNIC AREAS

RECREATION
FACILITIES
i.e. recreation center

BRIDAL TRAILS
access to WSTS

PAR COURSE / JOGGING

PLAYGROUND

AMPHITHEATER

ACTIVE
REC.

PARKING

LOT
#1

LOT
#2

ROAD TO WSTS

BOULEVARD

BUFFER

PASSIVE
RECREATION

PARKING

PICNIC AREAS

SCHEMATIC #1 / BUFFER PARK @
LANDER TECHNICAL PARK
LANDER, WYOMING.

MGA LANDPLANNERS
SCALE - 1" = 200'

N.

Exercise 16: FUNDAMENTAL DESIGN PHASES

a.   Redraw the examples of analysis, program and concept phases. Apply aspects of line control, quality and line weight variation. Also provide refined lettering.

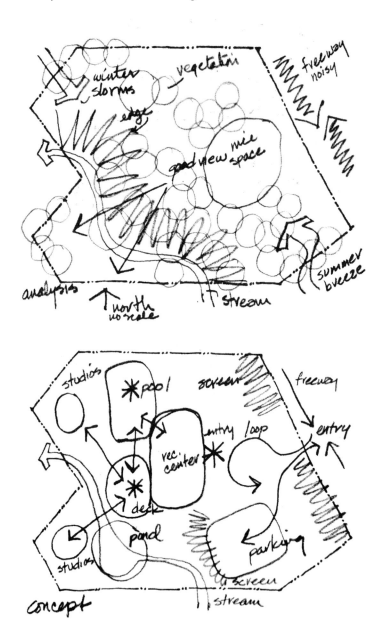

DESIGN DEVELOPMENT PHASES

Presentation of the more developed phases of the design process is also important. Because they show what the proposed design solution may actually look like when completed, a great deal of time and effort is normally spent on developing presentation graphics techniques. Unfortunately, many students waste their time and effort because they are unaware of some fundamental ideas related to presentation graphic technique.

A large part of presentation materials is portrayed as a two-dimensional image. However, most of the developed design ideas have three-dimensional characteristics. Therefore, representing the dimension of depth is necessary to create a sense of reality. Depth perception can be accomplished in a variety of ways. Three basic approaches are variation in line and value, overlapping elements, and spatial definition such as paraline and perspective images.

Another fundamental communication principle is based on the fact that some aspects of the design may be more important than others and, therefore, need to be emphasized. Graphic approaches to emphasizing these elements include variation in line and value and variation in detail. This approach will also give the information variety, yet maintain order. (See emphasis as a design principle, Chapter 2).

Simplicity is a basic communication principle that every beginning design student should consider. Often, in an effort to "polish" presentation information, students end up tarnishing a design idea with extensive rendering and graphic illustration. Simplicity in visual communication, as well as in design, is often the best approach.

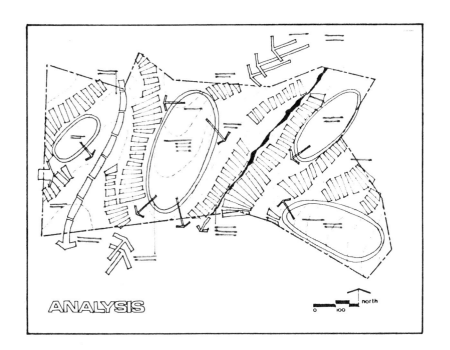

ANALYSIS

0 100 north

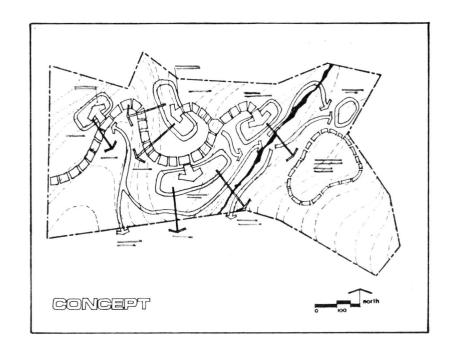

CONCEPT

0 100 north

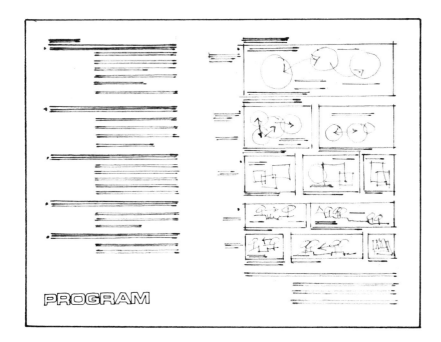

PROGRAM

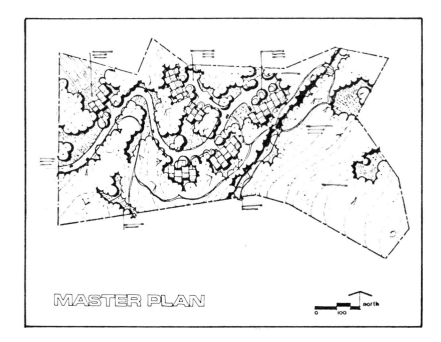

MASTER PLAN

0 100 north

Plan

Representative plan views are the most widely used of the graphics images because they quickly communicate design ideas in all phases of the design process. You might consider a few suggestions, therefore, when presenting plan view graphic information.

The scale of a plan view is, generally, related to the amount of detailed information that can be communicated. As a rule of thumb, remember that the larger the scale, the less detailed information necessary. Perhaps the point can be illustrated by describing plan view graphic scale with three scale categories:

Large Scale: 1″ = 60′ plus (approximate)

Large scale plans usually communicate large and comprehensive information. Building locations, tree massing, spatial relationships, and circulation modes are various examples of information described by large scale plan views.

Small Scale: 1″ = 20′ (approximate)

Small scale plan views are more able to communicate intricate detail and specific information. Planting plans, dimension plans, and other detailed construction design-graphics usually use a smaller scale.

Medium Scale: 1″ = 30′ to 1″ = 50′

Medium scale plan views are in a borderline category, where they could go either way depending on the situation. You should be able to decide which way to approach various medium scale plan views by following the suggestions already discussed.

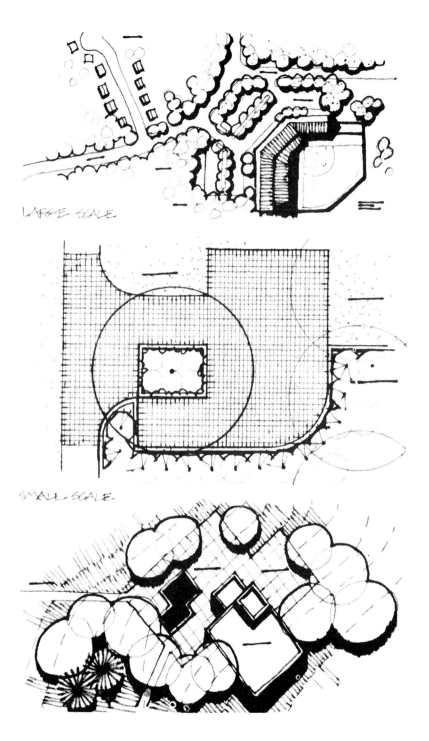

LARGE SCALE

SMALL SCALE

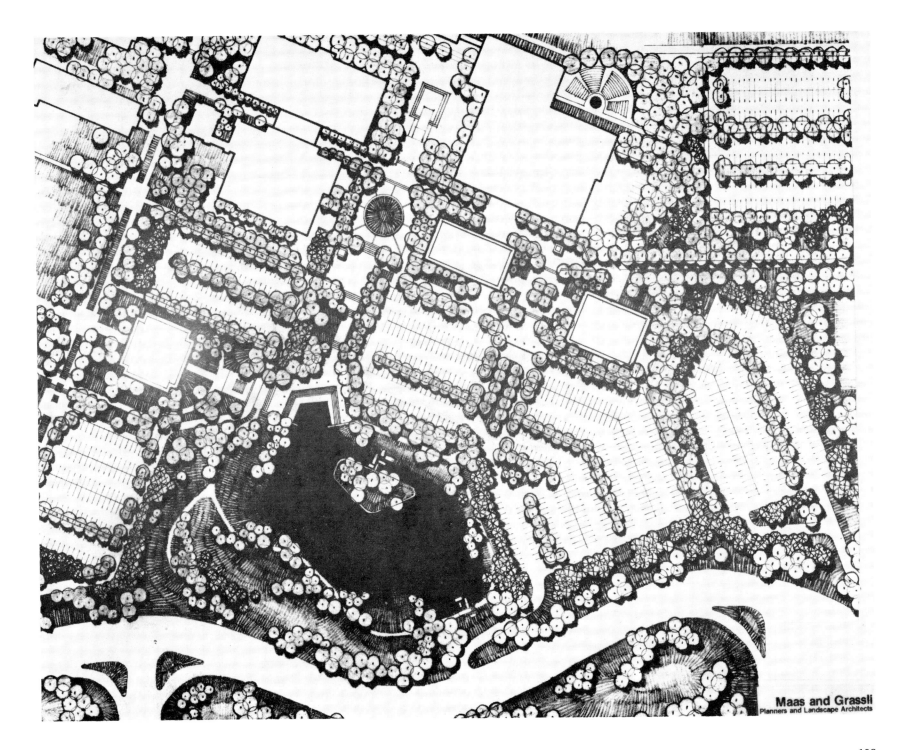

Maas and Grassli
Planners and Landscape Architects

109

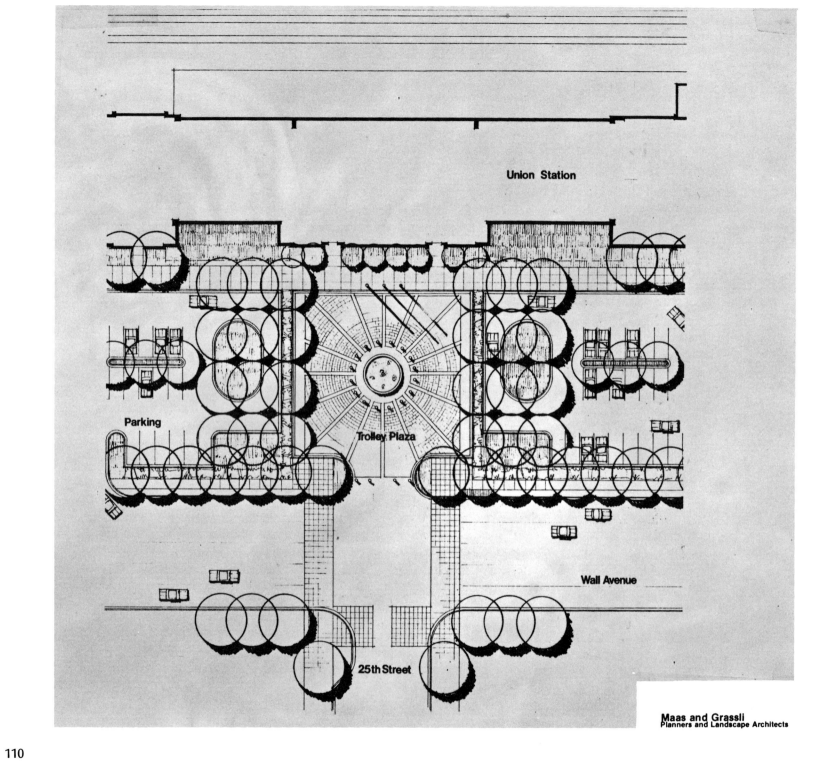

Union Station

Parking

Trolley Plaza

Wall Avenue

25th Street

Maas and Grassli
Planners and Landscape Architects

110

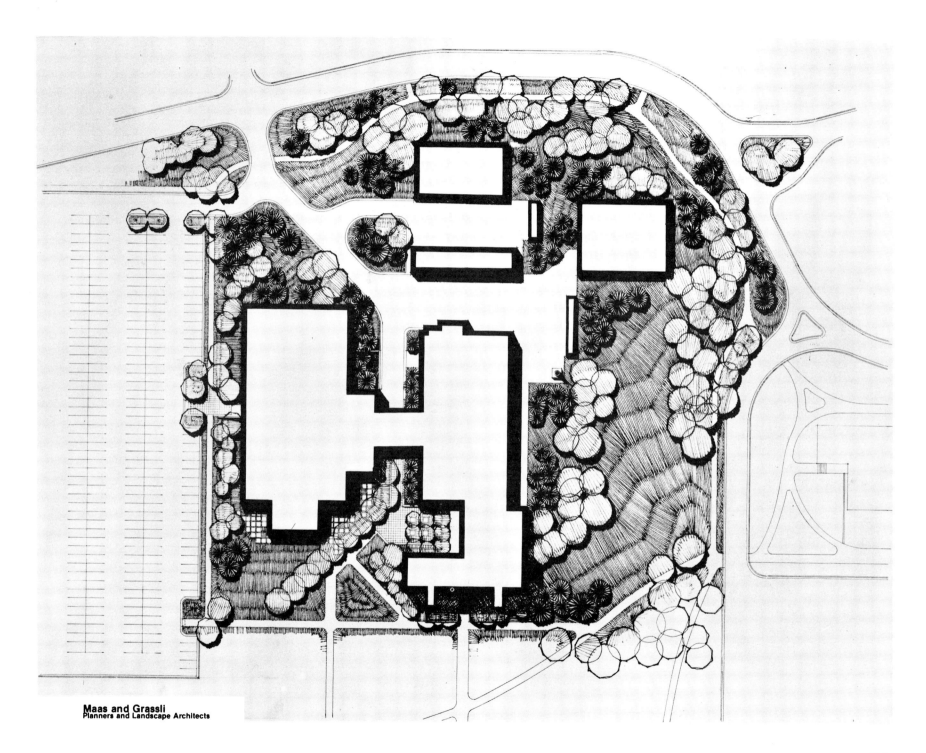

Maas and Grassli
Planners and Landscape Architects

111

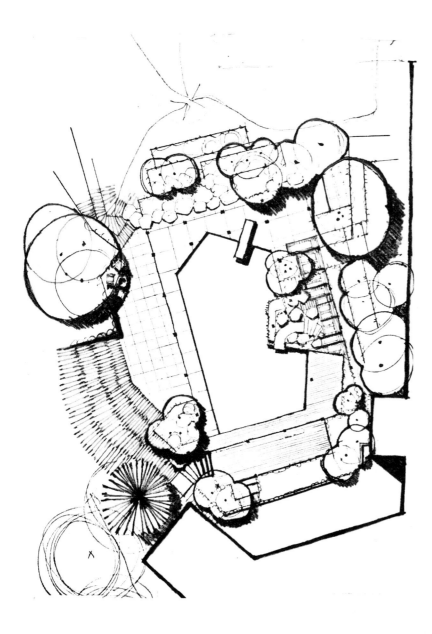

Creating perceptions of depth in plan view will help the image appear more realistic, and facilitate understanding of the plan view relationships. One approach to creating perceptions of depth is to vary the line weights of the elements in the plan. Ground elements should be thin and light, while those elements that would realistically be off the ground surface should be thicker and darker. Outlining buildings, trees, and other vertical elements in the plan view effectively creates this illusion of depth. It also helps emphasize the important elements and gives variety to the drawing. Using shadows in the plan view also effectively produces illusions of depth (see value, Chapter 7).

Rendering the plan view is also helpful in creating a realistic appearance to the project. However, simplicity is still best, especially if you are just beginning in design-graphics. When rendering a plan view remember it must first communicate design ideas.

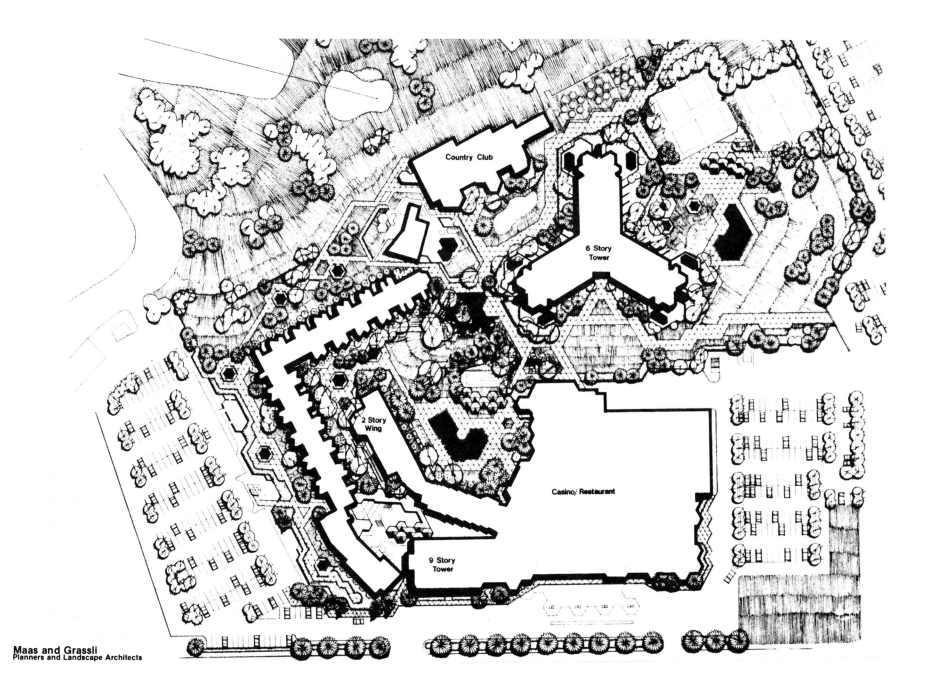

Country Club

6 Story
Tower

2 Story
Wing

Casino/ Restaurant

9 Story
Tower

Maas and Grassli
Planners and Landscape Architects

113

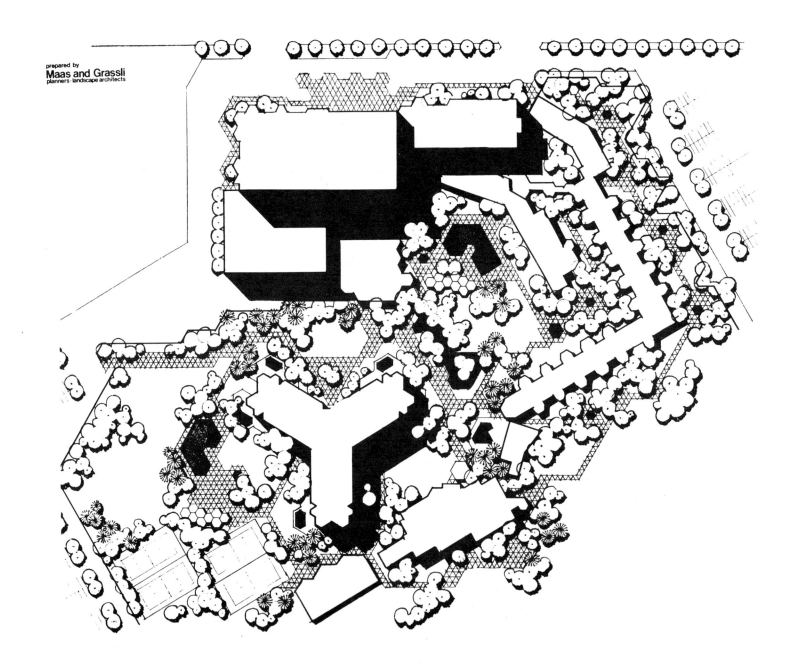

114

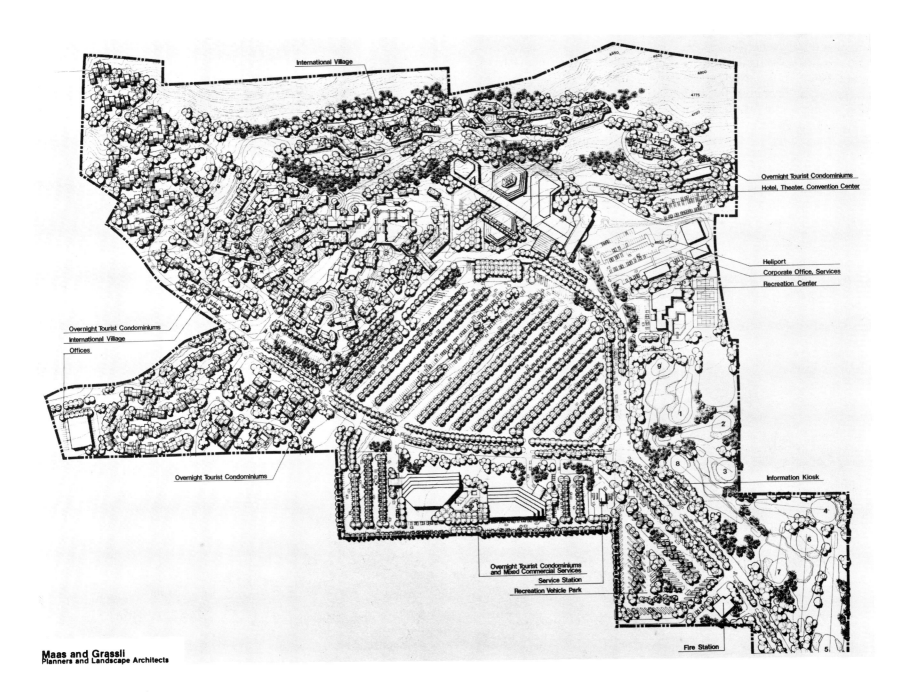

International Village

Overnight Tourist Condominiums
Hotel, Theater, Convention Center

Heliport
Corporate Office, Services
Recreation Center

Overnight Tourist Condominiums
International Village
Offices

Overnight Tourist Condominiums

Information Kiosk

Overnight Tourist Condominiums
and Mixed Commercial Services
Service Station
Recreation Vehicle Park

Fire Station

Maas and Grassli
Planners and Landscape Architects

115

Elevation

Representative elevation drawings offer another descriptive view of the proposed design solution. Elevations are often used to communicate building facades or other aspects of the design that have an interesting vertical-horizontal relationship.

Because elevations, like plans, are two-dimensional representations of three-dimensional ideas, you should utilize various graphic techniques that create the illusion of depth in the drawing. Depth perception is suggested in the same manner described for the plan view. The closer the elements would appear to the observer in reality, the darker and thicker the line weight should be drawn for those elements. Elements that would in reality appear further away are drawn with thin, light lines, and portray less detail. Use shadows and values as other approaches for suggesting depth (see Chapter 7).

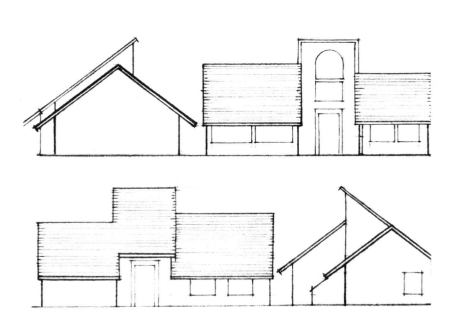

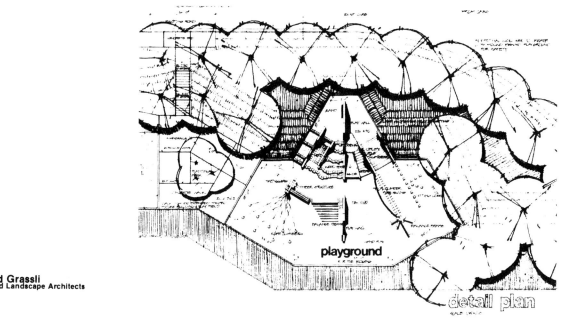

playground

detail plan

Maas and Grassli
Planners and Landscape Architects

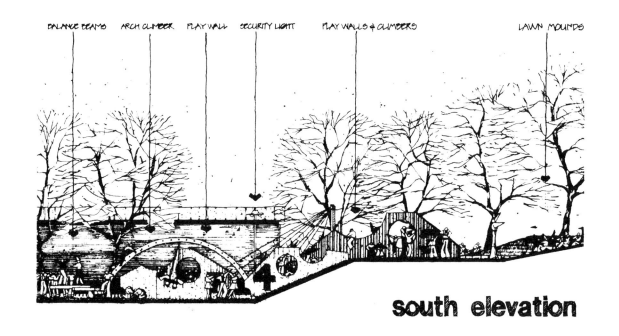

BALANCE BEAMS ARCH CLIMBER PLAY WALL SECURITY LIGHT PLAY WALLS & CLIMBERS LAWN MOUNDS

south elevation

117

Section

The section drawing is a very useful visual communication tool. It effectively describes the design idea by slicing through various parts of the design exposing the structural elements. It can be used in plan, elevation, or one of the three-dimensional images, paraline or perspective.

Plan section is simply the representation of the structural elements as they appear in plan view. Plan-sections are often used to explain the floor plan, or basic configuration of buildings.

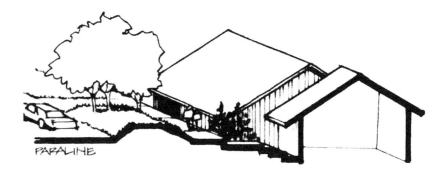

PARALINE

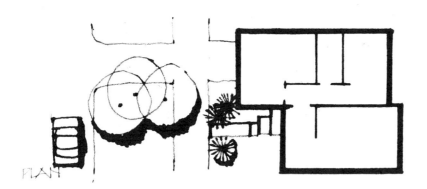

PLAN

Paraline and perspective section views create an image describing the spatial and structural relationships of a design idea. They are fairly easy to construct using the methods described in the paraline and perspective explanations (see Chapter 3).

PERSPECTIVE

Elevation section incorporates the aspects of the elevation with the qualities of the section and provides a view of the structural elements of the design as they relate to the vertical/horizontal elements. The section elevation is constructed in the same manner as the elevation.

ELEVATION

Exaggeration of the dimensions of a section is often useful to help explain the proportionate relationships of the design elements. For example, a section of the United States drawn with an exaggerated vertical dimension would describe the various land masses more easily than if both dimensions were precisely drawn. However, use exaggeration wisely, so as not to misrepresent precise information that may be needed, such as in construction documents (see Chapter 9).

PACIFIC | WEST COAST | ROCKIES | CENTRAL | APPAL. | EAST | ATLANTIC

EXAGGERATED VERTICALS

PACIFIC | WEST COAST | ROCKIES | CENTRAL | APPAL. | EAST | ATLANTIC

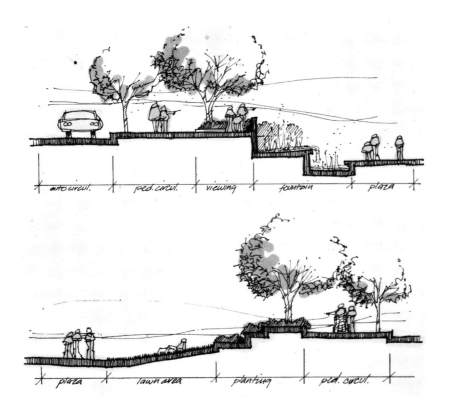

The creation of depth perception and emphasis of important design aspects as well as other graphic techniques already discussed for the plan and elevation, should be applied to representing the section.

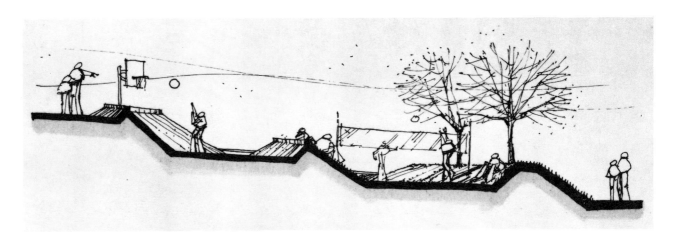

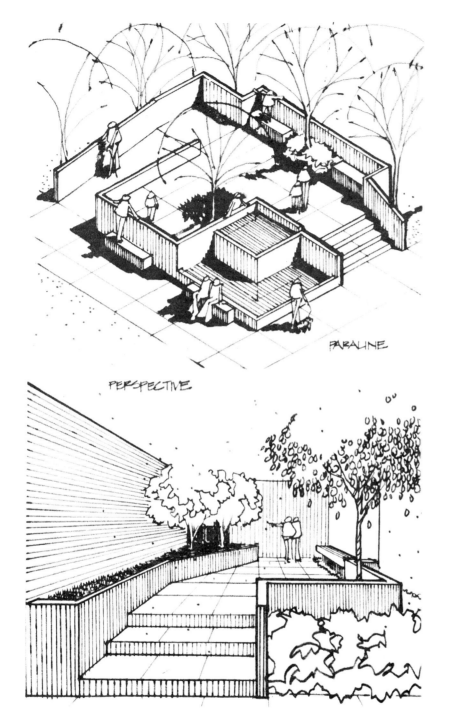

PARALINE

PERSPECTIVE

Paraline and Perspective

The three-dimensional qualities of the paraline and perspective images, enable them to represent design ideas with the greatest amount of spatial realism. These views are used quite extensively in presenting design solutions. They do, however, require more time to construct them and more consideration to present them effectively.

The use of line weight variation to enhance the perception of depth should not be neglected in illustrating these two forms, but should be conscientiously applied where emphasis is needed. In addition, variations in detail, value, and the use of shadow will help enhance the perception of depth in these drawings.

The key to utilizing the perspective and paraline images is knowing when they are needed and how to communicate them effectively. You will want to consider which view or angle of observation best describes your intentions. A view which obstructs the form of the design, for example, is not as effective as one that frames or emphasizes it.

Simplicity in rendering these images is also important to the overall presentation. Remember to strive for a balance between communicating essential information and rendering to create a sense of realism.

PREPLANNING

The key to preplanning your representative design information is to decide what may be important to communicate and how that information can best be conveyed. Preliminary ideas about format, lettering, organization and overall professional appearance of the final presentation should begin early in the design process. A few moments of foresight and preplanning may save hours of frustration and effort later on.

Consider what information you will want to include and how it can best be presented. For example, most site related information is portrayed with north at the top of the page. However, exceptions are possible if the slope of the site is more conducive to a horizontal orientation, with north to the right or left of the sheet.

Consider what information will need to be duplicated, and how to best make copies (see reproduction processes). Basemap information, for example, may be needed for a variety of presentation material. Format information, such as borderlines, title-blocks, or other aspects of a uniformed presentation can also be duplicated to save time and effort.

Work up a schematic diagram for your presentation information describing the format, types and organization of diagrams, charts, images, words, or anything else that may be included. Make rough tracing paper constructions of presentation ideas before committing them to the final work. In this way you may be able to better organize your information and evaluate your graphic approach before committing it to your final presentation material. Remember, however, that these should be quick and simple studies, and not refined illustrations. Too often students painstakingly render a trace study, only to repeat the same effort on the final copy.

Representation of information that doesn't require absolute accuracy should be portrayed quickly and often freehand. Using a circle template to draw a forest of plan view trees is an ineffective use of one's time.

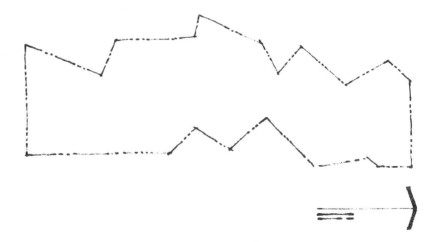

REPRODUCTION

Very often designers make a reproduction, or print, of a design-graphics idea. These prints are made by placing the original design idea (drawn on a translucent paper, such as trace), next to a light sensitive paper or film, and exposing them to light. The sensitive material will then retain an image where the light was blocked by the original image.

Some light sensitive materials are opaque papers and produce different colored lines, such as black, brown, or blue. These are most often used for presentation purposes and can easily be colored with markers or pencils.

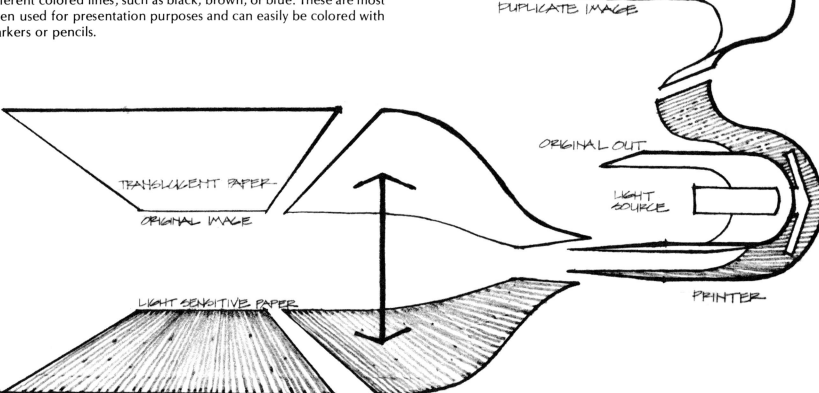

Other reproduction sensitive materials are translucent in composition and can be reused as a design-graphics original. These are particularly useful for duplicating information that is applicable to many different aspects of the presentation. For example, a basemap, north arrow, titleblock and borderline may be needed several times to describe one design solution. Utilization of these translucent prints enables you to duplicate this information quickly, supply the added information, and then produce the presentation final.

Other aspects of reproduction, such as reduction and enlargement of design ideas will also help you enhance your representative design-graphics skills. You should become very familiar with them and apply them to your design process. In many cases they can save you hours of time and energy.

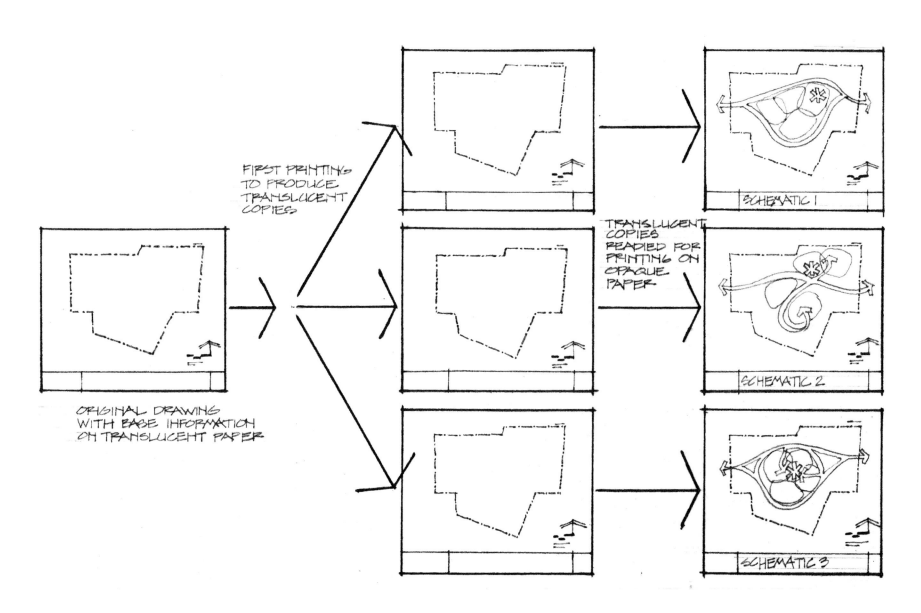

FIRST PRINTING TO PRODUCE TRANSLUCENT COPIES

ORIGINAL DRAWING WITH BASE INFORMATION ON TRANSLUCENT PAPER

TRANSLUCENT COPIES READIED FOR PRINTING ON OPAQUE PAPER

SCHEMATIC 1

SCHEMATIC 2

SCHEMATIC 3

Exercise 17: DESIGN DEVELOPMENT PHASES

a.   Redraw the given plan view using the appropriate linework and
      lettering. Add shadows as you desire.

b.   Create an elevation for one of the more interesting views of the
      plan.

c.   Create a section for the view indicated by the section line.
      Remember to exaggerate.

d.   Develop paraline images for the plan (isometric and oblique).

e.   Develop a one point and two point perspective for the image.

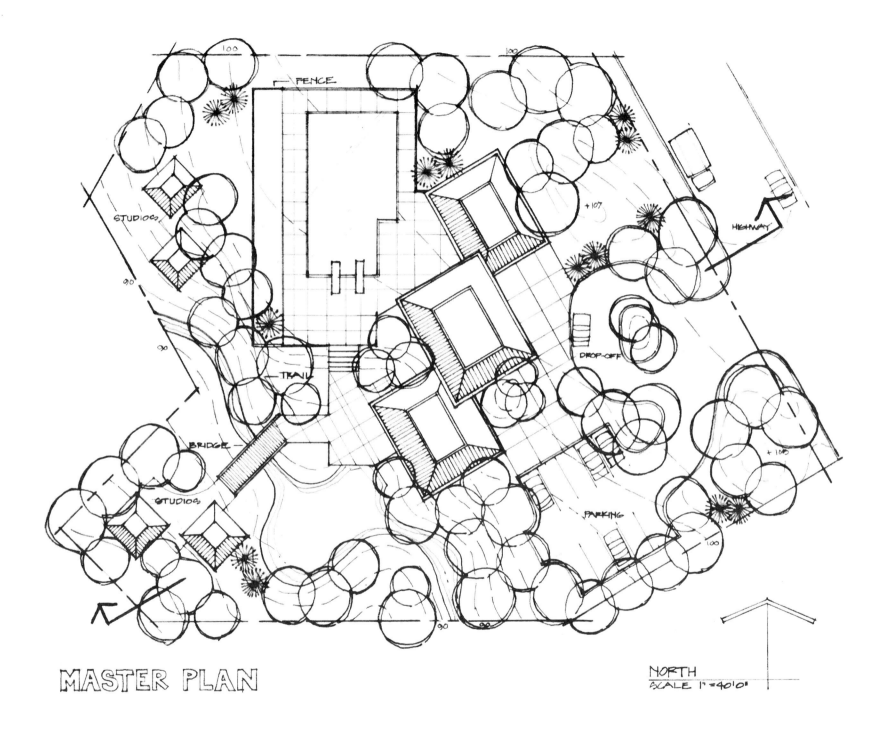

STUDIOS

FENCE

+ 107

HIGHWAY

DROP-OFF

TRAIL

BRIDGE

STUDIOS

PARKING

+ 100

MASTER PLAN

NORTH
SCALE 1"=40'0"

127

7

Visual Communication III

This chapter deals with other suggestions related to the more detailed aspects of visual communication and representative design-graphics that help to develop presentation ideas. The information presented here supports the previous two chapters, and this section should be viewed as adjunct to the earlier material. But without proper understanding the development of the principles of line, lettering, and look, the application of this information to your presentation graphics may be ineffective.

Much of the information discussed in this chapter is related to what might be considered basic drawing. It is intended to suggest approaches to developing basic drawing skills. The foremost suggestion for developing such skills, however, does not lie in the pages of a book, but in your personal effort. You should keep a sketchbook in which you can practice your basic graphic skills and develop your visual communication abilities.

SKETCHBOOK

The idea of keeping a sketchbook is bothersome for many because they often associate with it a sense of embarrassment in documenting their graphic ability. For example, many students neglect using their sketchbook because they feel they aren't able to draw and don't want others to see their work. Others seem to think that whatever goes into the sketchbook has to be a work of art, and therefore spend hours on a few very elaborate drawings. Remember that a sketch is a rapidly executed drawing. It refers to a preliminary or rough representation of ideas or designs. Therefore you should consider your sketchbook as the practice field for warming up drawing skills and developing design-graphics abilities. Quick and simple little doodles and graphic studies are examples of what should be drawn in a sketchbook. Certainly it may also contain more refined works, but you should mainly use it to refine the basic design-graphics techniques that you will need in the environmental design curriculum and profession.

Sketchings

Much of the information that has been discussed and presented in the book thus far is related to sketching. It represents what is a very fundamental design-graphics skill; quick and effective visual communication. Developing the ability to sketch stems from understanding the basic ideas and principles discussed in previous chapters on design and visual communication.

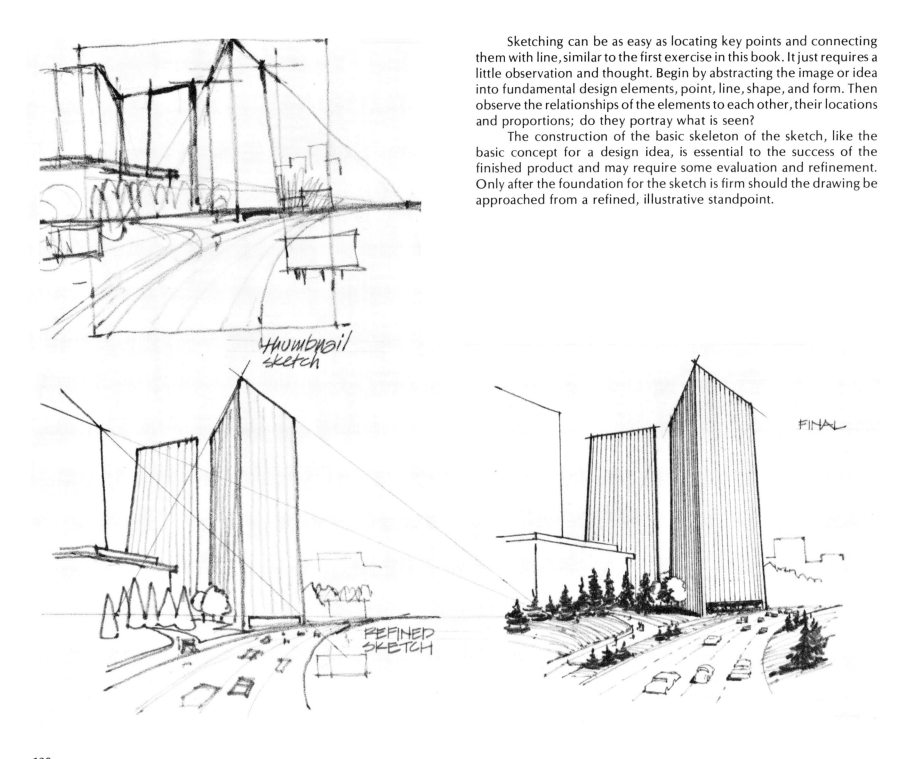

Sketching can be as easy as locating key points and connecting them with line, similar to the first exercise in this book. It just requires a little observation and thought. Begin by abstracting the image or idea into fundamental design elements, point, line, shape, and form. Then observe the relationships of the elements to each other, their locations and proportions; do they portray what is seen?

The construction of the basic skeleton of the sketch, like the basic concept for a design idea, is essential to the success of the finished product and may require some evaluation and refinement. Only after the foundation for the sketch is firm should the drawing be approached from a refined, illustrative standpoint.

thumbnail sketch

REFINED SKETCH

FINAL

The key to sketching is seeing. It is part of the eye-hand-mind relationship that is so important to design-graphics communication. You will need to develop the ability to represent images *as they appear,* not as you know them to be. For example, young children, unaware of the principles of perspective, often portray a house as being very flat, almost orthographic, because they know that a house is composed of horizontal and vertical walls and windows. Too often adults draw with the same approach. They look at the object once, see that it is a house, and then draw a house as they remember it from their childhood.

Doodling

Although doodling is often associated with idleness, it has an important function in the design profession where the term means either "relaxed drawing" or concentration on random drawing ability and visual communication technique. A large portion of the sketchbook should be devoted to doodling and experimenting with the various graphic approaches that are suggested in this book and other graphic texts. Doodling should be purposeful and relaxed in order to be effective.

SUPPORT IMAGES

The use of cars, people, plants and other images that help support a design idea are very important to the communication of presentation information for a number of reasons. First, they give a sense of scale to the drawings, a reference of the size and relationship of design elements. They also give additional definition to the various uses and purposes of the design. For example, cars suggest auto circulation.

The example shows support images rendered in different styles and techniques to demonstrate the variety of possibilities. These figures are intended to act as models from which you can develop your own rendering styles. Each technique, however, is related to a particular visual communication approach, of which you should be aware when applying it to your work. Do not simply select technique haphazardly. Try to understand why and how the particular technique was used. Too often students utilize various examples of graphic images on a smorgasbord fashion and wind up with goulash.

Figures can be easily drawn by blocking in their various proportions and smoothing off the edges. Notice the diagram that demonstrates these proportions and the blocking technique applied to different figure positions. You should begin to develop your abilities to represent figures in a variety of positions and graphic levels. Initially you may even want to collect photographs of figures from magazines and trace the image onto your presentation drawing.

Figures

The scale figure is perhaps the most useful of the support images because of the humanization and realism it gives a presentation drawing. The important thing to remember when developing figures, is that they are usually only supportive and don't require a lot of detail or refinement. They should, however, portray some proportionate and living qualities, if they are to be effective.

Vegetation

The use of vegetation in representing design ideas is also very effective in humanizing a drawing. In some case it may be the key element of the design idea itself and not simply a support element (see Chapter 8). In any case it is important to develop your ability to portray vegetation for presentation purposes.

Proportion is again a fundamental aspect of creating various vegetative images. The relationships of the branches, stems, trunks and leaves to the overall form are critical. Use your analytical approach to seeing the environment to help identify these relationships more clearly.

Trees grow from the ground up to the sky. A very basic technique for creating tree forms is to begin every stroke from the base and extend it out to the twigs. Trees are broad at the base and become gradually thinner as they develop. Notice the proportions of the trunk, the branches and the twigs in the examples.

Another approach to drawing trees is to block in the basic form. Again, be aware of the proportions. Notice how the canopy size is relative to the trunk diameter.

Shrubs can be drawn in a variety of different ways. Often it is simply a scaled-down version of a tree form. In the following examples of shrubs, as well as the trees, notice how the various textures and values are related to the use of line and shape. Also notice that many of the forms are simply implied.

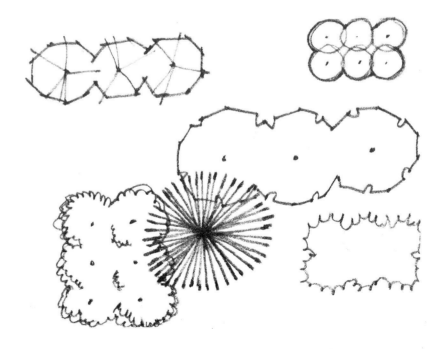

135

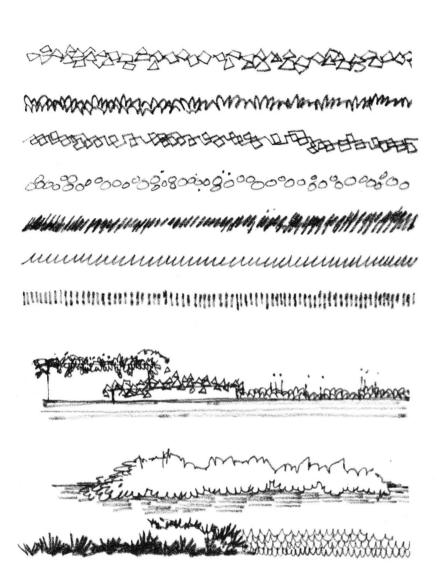

Other Accessories

Cars, boats, planes, animals, and any other images that may support the communication of a design idea are very important to develop as a part of your presentation portfolio. Apply the principles of proportion and detail to these in the same way that they applied to the other support images.

Ground cover and grass texture is easily drawn by simple expressions of line and shape. Notice the relationship between the proportions of the lines and shapes and the scale of the drawing. Also notice that the detail of the image for many of these techniques relates to a different style or graphic technique. The more detailed the information about the image, the more refined and illustrative the technique.

VALUE

Value is a relationship of lightness and darkness. In the environment the perception of values is useful in defining the various forms and relationships that exist. In representing design ideas it is helpful in defining these forms and relationships. It can be used to define differences in color or the reflective qualities of different materials. Variations in value can also create the illusion of depth and help emphasize design ideas in presentation graphics.

Various techniques are utilized in developing values. Many simply use line or points. Others are accomplished by rubbing the graphite over the drawing to create a wash effect. Still other values are created by applying textures.

Depth Perception and Detail

As another rule of thumb, remember that those elements that would in reality appear closer to the observer, should have a darker value than similar elements that would appear further away. In the same respect, detail of values would be more refined for those elements that would appear closer to the observer.

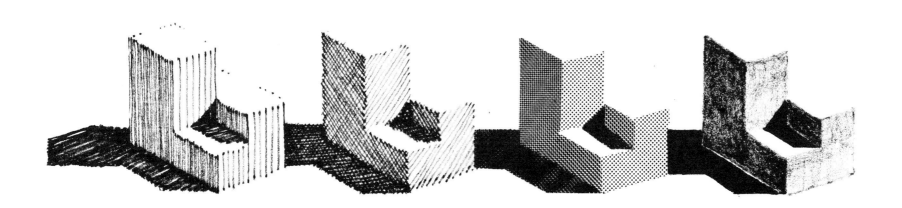

137

LINE

LINE AS VALUES

138

Shade and Shadow

Simply speaking, shade is the value of surfaces directly or indirectly influenced by light, while shadow is the value or image on a surface created by blocking out light. Both are very important and require consideration and thought to be effective in presenting design information. Actual calculations of sun angle, azimuth, and altitude are useful in creating very precise drawings of shade and shadow. However, a fundamental understanding of shade and shadow will be most beneficial and will allow you to present ideas more quickly and skillfully.

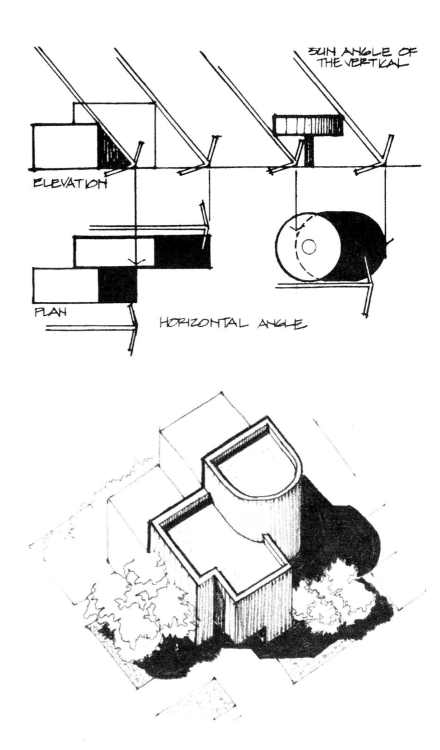

SUN ANGLE OF THE VERTICAL

ELEVATION

PLAN

HORIZONTAL ANGLE

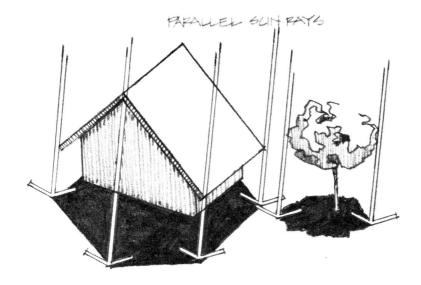

PARALLEL SUN RAYS

Values on different surfaces are relative to the amount of light that is absorbed by the surface. Those surfaces furthest from the direct source will usually have the darker value. The shadow will also relate to the light source and be directly opposite. Consider the following examples and notice how the use of variations in value helps define the various surfaces.

139

Shadows define the location of the light source and the image that casts the shadow. Shadows also define the relationships of various images to each other. Notice how the shadows in the examples vary relative to the height of the surfaces that receive the shadow. Knowledge of this fact can create the illusion of depth in your drawings and help communicate design elements more effectively.

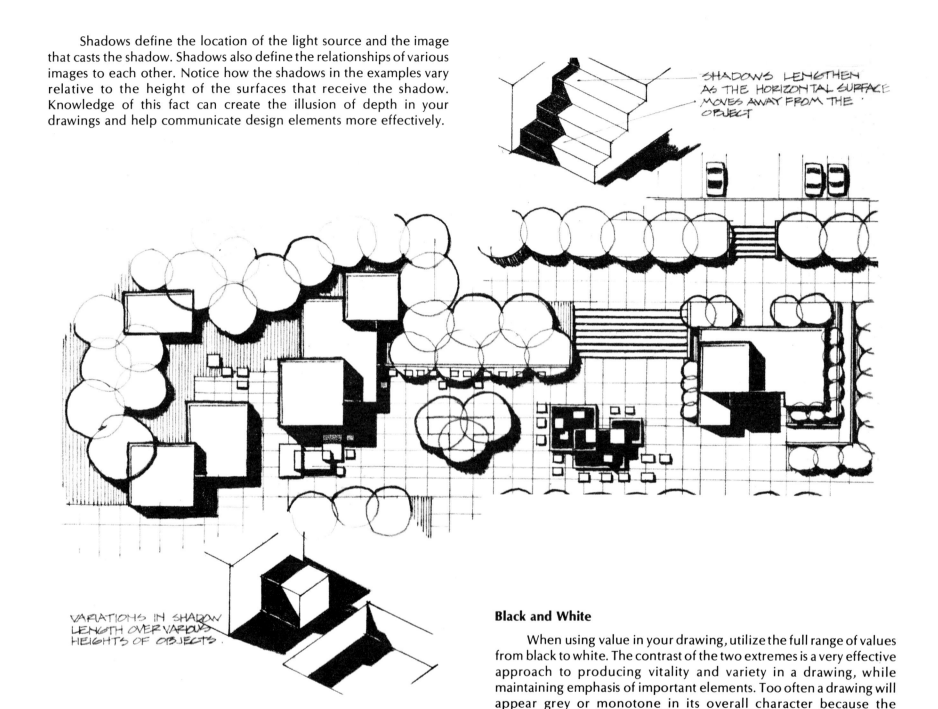

SHADOWS LENGTHEN AS THE HORIZONTAL SURFACE MOVES AWAY FROM THE OBJECT

VARIATIONS IN SHADOW LENGTH OVER VARIOUS HEIGHTS OF OBJECTS.

Black and White

When using value in your drawing, utilize the full range of values from black to white. The contrast of the two extremes is a very effective approach to producing vitality and variety in a drawing, while maintaining emphasis of important elements. Too often a drawing will appear grey or monotone in its overall character because the delineator did not utilize the full range of values.

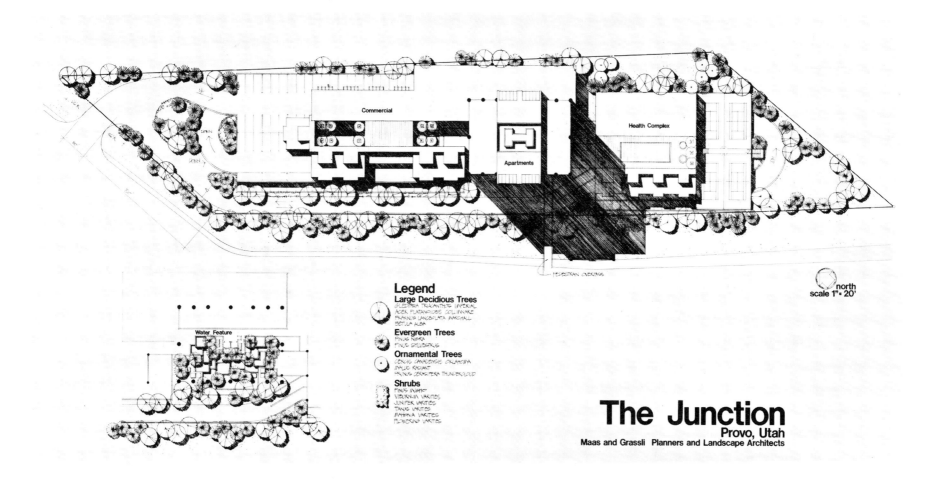

Commercial

Health Complex

Apartments

PEDESTRIAN OVERPASS

Legend

Large Decidious Trees
GLEDITSIA TRIACANTHOS IMPERIAL
ACER PLATANOIDES COLUMNARE
FRAXINUS LANCEOLATA MARSHALL
BETULA ALBA

Evergreen Trees
PINUS NIGRA
PINUS SYLVESTRIS

Ornamental Trees
CERCIS CANADENSIS OKLAHOMA
MALUS RADIANT
PRUNUS CERASIFERA THUNDERCLOUD

Shrubs
PINUS MUGHO
VIBURNUM VARITIES
JUNIPER VARITIES
TAXUS VARITIES
MAHONIA VARITIES
FLOWERING VARITIES

north
scale 1"= 20'

Water Feature

The Junction
Provo, Utah
Maas and Grassli Planners and Landscape Architects

TEXTURE

Texture, like value, can communicate the more detailed aspects of a proposed design solution. It can describe plant or construction materials, surfaces, patterns, and a variety of other characteristics related to your design ideas.

When applying texture to your drawings, remember that too many textures can create confusion and competition for emphasis. Utilize texture rendering in your representative design-graphics to enhance the intended purpose behind the idea. Often it is difficult to understand the main idea behind an illustration because the illustrative approach is so overpowering.

Maas and Grassli
Planners and Landscape Architects

Exercise 18: SKETCHBOOK and SUPPORT IMAGERY

a. Obtain and use a sketchbook.

b. Practice your graphic technique in all aspects of the design-graphics relationship.

c. Collect examples of quality graphic technique, and trace them. After a while you will develop your own style of graphic communication.

d. Apply various textures, values, support images, etc., to the line image given to the right.

REFERENCES

The following is a list of recommended books that support the information presented in the previous section.

Atkin, W.W., 1976. *Architectural Presentation.* New York: Van Nostrand Reinhold. 196 pages.

Ching, F., 1975. *Architectural Graphics.* New York: Van Nostrand Reinhold. 128 pages.

Doyle, M.E., 1981. *Color Drawing.* New York: Van Nostrand Reinhold. 320 pages.

Forseth, K., Baughan, D., 1980. *Graphics for Architects.* New York: Van Nostrand Reinhold. 223 pages.

Jacoby, H., 1971. *New Techniques of Architectural Rendering.* New York: Praeger.

Kliment, S.A., 1977. *Creative Communications for a Successful Design Practice.* New York: Watson-Guptill Pub. 192 pages.

Martin, C.L., 1968. *Design Graphics.* New York: MacMillan.

Murgio, M., 1969. *Communication Graphics.* New York: Van Nostrand Reinhold. 240 pages.

Oles, P.S., *Architectural Illustration – The Value Delineation Process.* New York: Van Nostrand Reinhold. 275 pages.

Porter, T., Greenstreet, B., 1980. *Manual of Graphic Techniques.* New York: Charles Scribner's and Sons.

Porter T., Goodman, S., 1984. *Manual of Graphic Techniques 4.* New York: Charles Scribner's and Sons. 128 pages.

Thiel, P., 1965. *Freehand Drawing.* Seattle, WA: University of Washington Press. 127 pages.

Vrooman, D., 1983. *Architecture: Perspective Shadows and Reflections.* New York: Van Nostrand Reinhold. 152 pages.

Walker, T.D., 1982. *Perspective Sketches.* 4th Edition. Mesa, AZ: PDA Publishers. 250 pages.

Walker, T.D., 1985. *Plan Graphics.* 3rd Edition, Mesa, AZ: PDA Publishers. 235 pages.

Wang, T., 1977. *Pencil Sketching.* New York: Van Nostrand Reinhold.

Wang, T., 1979. *Plan and Section Drawing.* New York: Van Nostrand Reinhold. 96 pages.

SECTION C

CONSTRUCTION DESIGN-GRAPHICS

This section of the book deals with the final level of the design-graphics communication relationship. It describes the refinement of design ideas and the graphic communication of those ideas to interested persons who will use them.

Once the proposed design solution has been represented, evaluated by the client, refined and accepted, it must then go through a final refinement process during which the construction documents are produced. These documents, often called "working drawings," are the means by which the design solution becomes reality. The information they contain enables a contractor to understand how to build a design project as intended by the designer.

The information provided in this section should help you develop an understanding of the basic characteristics of construction design-graphics and its relationship to the design process. You will, of necessity, want to develop your abilities in this area, as you will undoubtedly be required to prepare construction drawings as part of the environmental design curriculum and profession.

Utilize the information presented in this book, as well as additional information from other sources that will help in the development of your construction design-graphics ability.

8
Technical Communication I

Construction design-graphics relates to the final phase of the design process, the construction phase. It refers to the very detailed and technical communication of ideas needed to build the design.

The graphic approach to this technical communication is what might be referred to as drafting. Drafting suggests an accurate and precise description of visual information. Most often mechanical drawing instruments are utilized in order to ensure this precision, however, there are instances when construction drawings are drawn freehand.

The level of refinement of these drawings is obviously greater than that of the previous sections. Nevertheless, the principle objectives of these drawings, like those of the other two sections, are the same; quick and effective communication of design ideas. In this chapter several aspects of technical communication are suggested which are fundamental to accomplishing those objectives.

LINE

Line is the primary element in the design-graphics relationship. At this level of graphic refinement, the line, and consideration for line control and quality, is essential.

Because the information presented in working drawings is duplicated by means of reproduction printing, the quality of the original must be excellent in order to make quality reproductions. Suppose for example, that a key line of the drawing were drawn haphazardly with little concern for control or quality. The photo reproduction of the line may not duplicate the line accurately and the entire construction of the design might be thrown off.

Accuracy in delineation at the construction graphics level is critical. You should try to make all your lines as uniform and consistent as possible. Object lines that describe a square, for example, should be drawn with the same density and width for each of the four sides. The alignment and connection of lines is also important to the quality of the drawings. Tangents and circles, and other intersection of lines, should portray accuracy and line control.

Line weight variation is particularly important in communicating quality construction drawings. Because construction drawings can be complex and intricate in line, variation of the line weight can produce a hierarchy of line that enables easy comprehension of different line meanings. The hierarchy is usually structured so that the aspects of the drawing which are more important, such as object lines and section lines, are bolder and darker than those aspects that are supportive or descriptive, such as dimension and extension lines. Guidelines and preliminary construction lines are used specifically for reference and should be thin and very light (see line, Chapter 5).

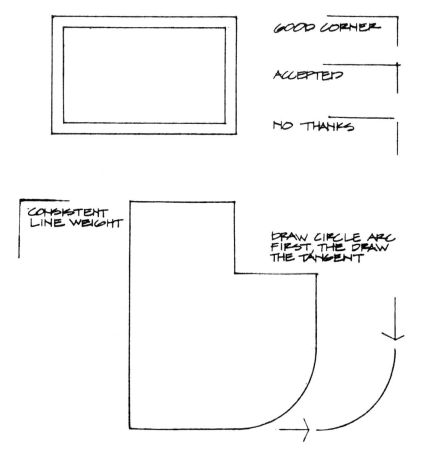

150

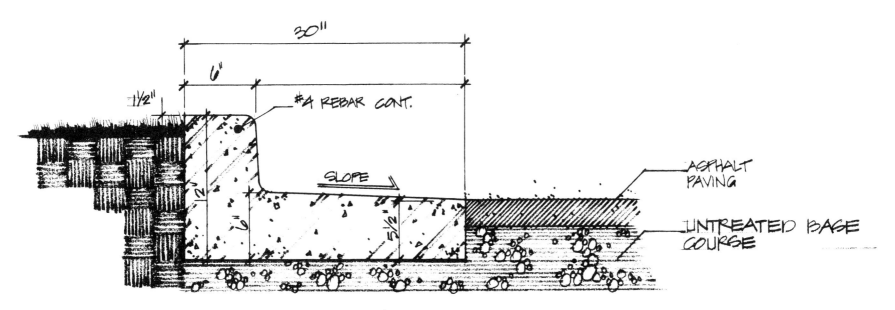

30"

6"

1½"

#4 REBAR CONT.

SLOPE

12

6

5½

ASPHALT PAVING

UNTREATED BASE COURSE

NOTE : CONSTRUCT ALL CURB & GUTTER WITH PAN
JOINTS EVERY 10'-0" O.C. AND ½" EXPANSION JOINTS
EVERY 20'-0" O.C. INSTALL 2- #4 ⌀ GREASED DOWELS
X 24" AT ALL EXPANSION JOINTS. ALL PAN JOINTS THAT
SPAN A TRENCH OR EXCAVATED AREA, INSTALL 2- #4
REBAR. IN AREAS OF FILL COMPACT SUB -BASE
MATERIAL TO 95% OF LABORATORY DENSITY IN
ACCORDANCE W/ ASTM D 1557-70.

TYPICAL CURB & GUTTER DETAIL
SCALE   1½" = 1'-0"

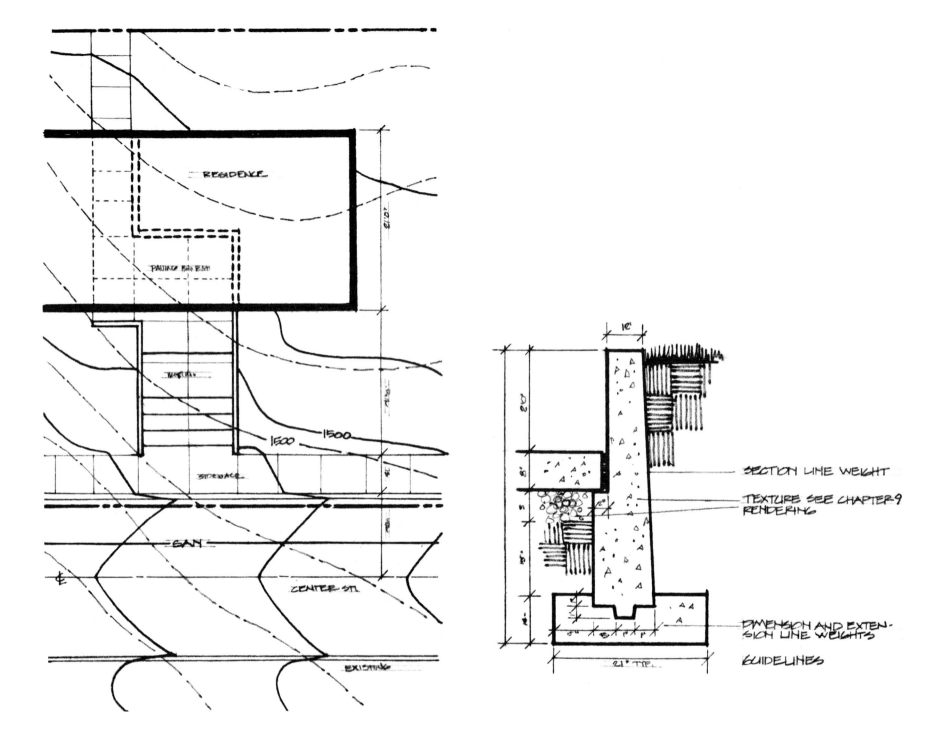

RESIDENCE

PATIO BR 8.5'

WARTALL

1500   1500

SIDEWALK

GAN

CENTER STL

EXISTING

SECTION LINE WEIGHT

TEXTURE SEE CHAPTER 9
RENDERING

DIMENSION AND EXTEN-
SION LINE WEIGHTS

GUIDELINES

LOOK

The look of the construction drawings, like the presentation drawings, is very important to the communication of information. Most of the aspects of look discussed in Chapter 5 are also applicable with regard to technical communication skills. This section reiterates some of those aspects and suggests others that are especially significant.

The size and complexity of a design project will undoubtedly effect the amount and complexity of the technical information needed to construct the project. A large project may include information about layout, dimensions, grading, drainage, planting and sprinkling, each having detailed information explaining how it is to be built. This information is compiled into what is often called a "construction drawing package." The format and general organization of the package is important to maintain uniformity and simple communication of design ideas.

Construction packages are usually organized in a horizontal format, with titleblocks and borderlines. An extra large margin on the left-hand side of the drawing sheets is used for binding the various sheets of information together. Space is provided on the sheet, usually as part of the titleblock, for the numbering of the sheets. An index and cover sheet is also included as part of the package.

BORDERLINES AND TITLE BLOCKS.

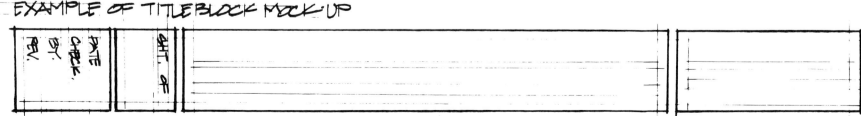

EXAMPLE OF TITLEBLOCK MOCK-UP

LETTERING

Contractors who are responsible for the construction of a design project are not always familiar with the intentions of the designer. The written information that accompanies the graphic images, therefore, is very important to explain these intentions. This implies that the legibility and quality of the lettering of a construction drawing is also essential for quick and effective technical communication.

Very often a construction drawing will require as much written information as it does graphic. A custom design for a playground, for example, will need to specify virtually everything about the materials and procedures that are required to build it. Most of this information will need to be explained in written form. For this reason you should learn to work in a rapid and readable freehand lettering style.

The organization and placement of the lettering is also critical to clear communication. Make sure that your lettering relates easily to the object it describes. Organize and locate your lettering in such a way that it will clarify the drawing, not clutter it. Leader lines that relate words to images also need to be organized to avoid confusion. Avoid crossing leader lines whenever possible.

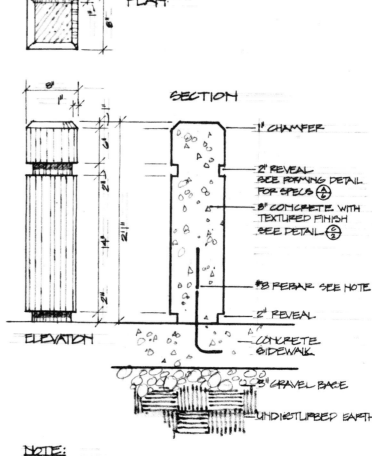

154

PREPLANNING

The preliminary development and preplanning of the construction drawings is a very significant aspect of technical communication. Not only will it enhance the quality of the drawings, but it will also reduce your time in preparing them. Prepare your information on tracing paper in a very rough form at first. Then when you begin to organize your sheets, place the tracings under the final drawing sheet (complete with borderlines, titleblock, etc.) and carefully trace the information as a refined image.

Other approaches to preliminary layouts include using light construction lines (similar to lettering guidelines) or non-print blue pencils to organize the various pieces of information.

The organization or the composition of the information on the individual sheets is also very important. Try to locate related pieces of information, such as a plan and section view for the same object, close enough to make easy comparisons and relationships between the two.

Titling the various aspects of the information and cross referencing is also important. Once again, remember to incorporate qualities of good lettering to make the information legible.

Construction drawings are often read out-of-doors, in the worst of conditions, and by a variety of contractors. Make sure that the drawings communicate the information in a clear, concise and accurate fashion, so that the contractors will be able to perform their part in the design process quickly and effectively.

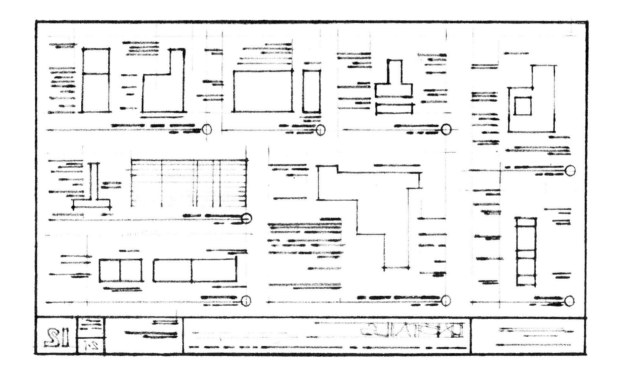

9
Technical
Communication
II

This chapter deals with several specific applications of the material discussed in the preceding chapter. It provides additional understanding of construction design-graphics and technical communication techniques related to construction drawings. Several of the more commonly used construction drawings are briefly discussed, and examples are provided to illustrate important points.

Technical communication, like other forms of graphic communication discussed in this book, has no standard rules. It is based on the fundamental principle that the designer should understand what is important to communicate, and know how that information can best be conveyed. There are, however, standard approaches and graphic techniques used in construction drawings which facilitate communication of design ideas between the various professions involved. The information presented in this book is patterned after those standards, but should not be considered as a source for them. The books listed in the reference sections provide much more comprehensive coverage of design techniques and standards.

CROSS REFERENCES AND LEGENDS

Most of the technical information presented in a construction drawing package comes in the form of a plan or related details. Because many aspects of the design cannot be completely understood by reading the plan, cross references are made to these details which explain where to locate specific and detailed information about the design construction.

Also included are legends which explain the graphic symbols of the drawings, and any additional notes that suggest how the design is to be constructed.

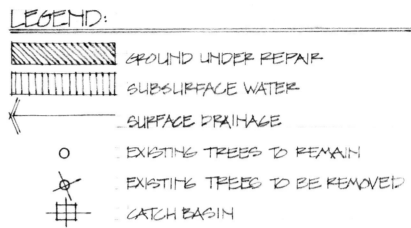

LEGEND:

GROUND UNDER REPAIR

SUBSURFACE WATER

SURFACE DRAINAGE

O EXISTING TREES TO REMAIN

EXISTING TREES TO BE REMOVED

CATCH BASIN

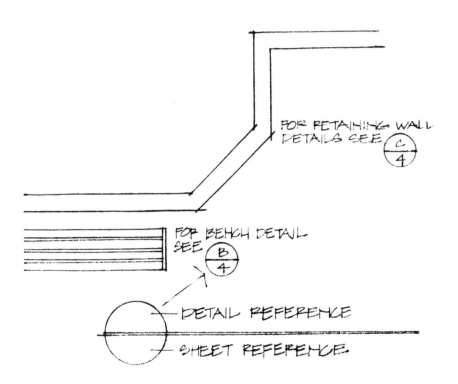

FOR RETAINING WALL DETAILS SEE C/4

FOR BENCH DETAIL SEE B/4

DETAIL REFERENCE

SHEET REFERENCE

NOTES:

ALL STAKING LOCATIONS TO BE APPROVED BY LANDSCAPE ARCHITECT.
SEE ARCHITECTURE DRAWINGS FOR STRUCTURES
SEE ENGINEERING PLAN FOR UTILITY LOCATIONS
PROJECT LIMIT LINES ARE APPROXIMATE ONLY CONTRACTORS WILL GO BEYOND LIMITS WHEN NECESSARY TO MEET EXISTING CONDITIONS, CONNECT UTILITIES, OR TO COMPLETE THE INTENTIONS OF THE LANDSCAPE ARCHITECT.
SEE DETAILS FOR SCHEDULES AND SPECS FOR ALL RETAINING WALLS
ALL WRITTEN DIMENSIONS PREVAIL
ALL EXPANSION JOINTS NOT TO EXCEED 5'0" IN RETAINING WALLS

COVER SHEET AND ORGANIZATION

The organization of the construction package should correspond to the sequence of the actual construction. Usually the package is arranged with the layout plan first, followed by dimensions, grades, construction details, and, finally, the planting plan and details.

A cover sheet that acts as an index and title page is added, and the entire construction drawing package is bound on the left-hand margin.

Layout Plan

The layout plan identifies the structural framework of the proposed design construction. It usually includes information related to existing conditions and proposed structural features such as buildings, retaining walls, paving, edges, major plant materials and circulation modes. Property lines, construction limit lines, and sheet match lines, are other elements often included as part of the layout plan.

Cross referencing details related to the structural features of the layout plan are also important, as are any additional notes or references which will help explain how the structural framework is to be laid out.

In many instances the information included on the layout drawing is useful in describing other plan drawings as well. Preplanning the layout so the drawing can be duplicated and used as a base plan can be a very effective time saving approach (see reproductions, Chapter 6).

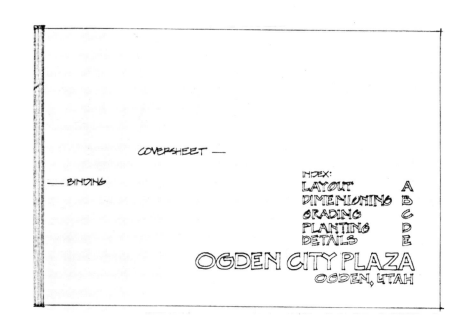

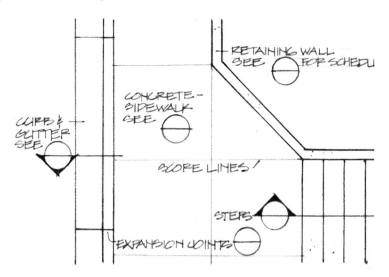

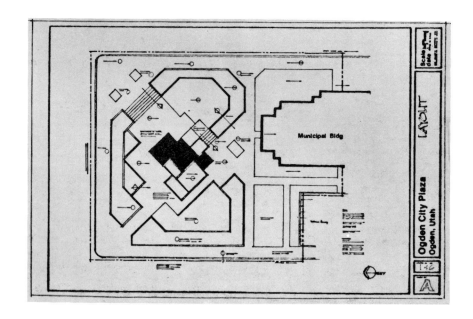

158

Dimensioning Plan

The dimensions of the proposed design and the relationship of new construction to existing conditions, is often included in the layout plan. In some cases it is presented on a separate drawing called the dimensioning plan. The accuracy and communication of measurements in dimensioning plans and related details is absolutely essential.

Dimensions in a drawing are indicated along a solid "dimension line" that is related to the object by "extension lines." Dimension lines should never be crisscrossed except where absolutely necessary. All dimensions should read from the bottom or right side of the sheet relative to the object. They should not be placed in shaded or textured areas.

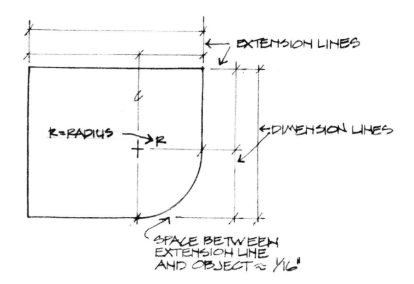

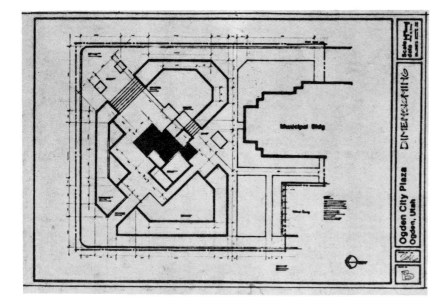

Quality lettering of the dimensions is absolutely vital. Dimensions are written in increments of an inch up to a foot, and in feet and inch values for greater distances. The inch and foot symbols, as well as any points on the drawing, should be distinct enough that they are not confused with specks on the print.

"R" is an indication of the radius of a circle and "D" the diameter. Both should proceed the actual dimension.

Because reproduction processes involved in duplicating construction drawings often alter the actual lengths and measurements of scale, dimensioning becomes the primary reference for construction. Due to these alterations, often the note "DO NOT SCALE" or "NOT TO SCALE," is indicated for information related to calculated measurements.

Grading Plan

The grading plan identifies the existing and proposed elevations and contour of the design project. Existing contour lines are indicated by dashed lines or dots, and should be drawn lighter than the proposed contour lines which are bold solid lines. Spot elevations of buildings, steps, walls and other features are also included. Occasionally grading plans will also include drainage flow and indicate the removal of existing features that are not desired as part of the design.

Line weight variation and lettering is extremely important to effectively communicate the grading plan, especially when a duplicate base map is used. Remember that the base map is only a reference and is supportive of the grading information which should be emphasized.

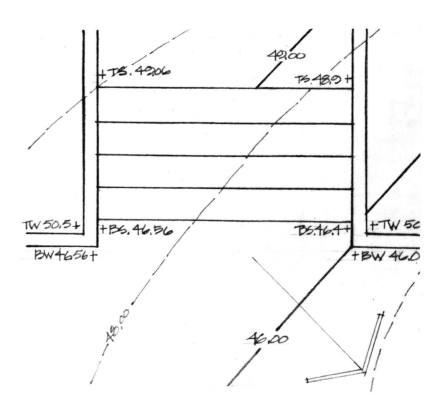

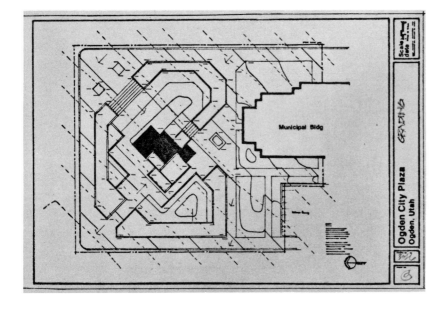

Planting Plan

The planting plan identifies the various vegetative elements that are proposed for design construction. Trees and shrubs are usually located by their centers. Lines that indicate foliage should be merely supportive of the plant locations and drawn very lightly. Ground covers and grasses are usually represented by a value or simple texture.

Quality lettering is again important in describing the name and number of the plant material proposed. Leader lines, connecting materials and written information, should be easily followed.

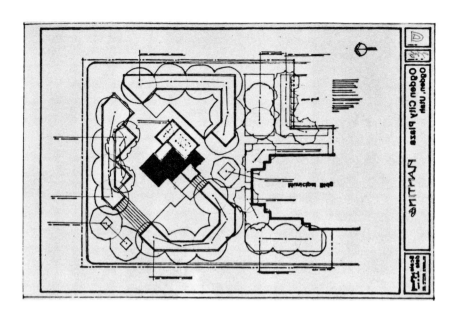

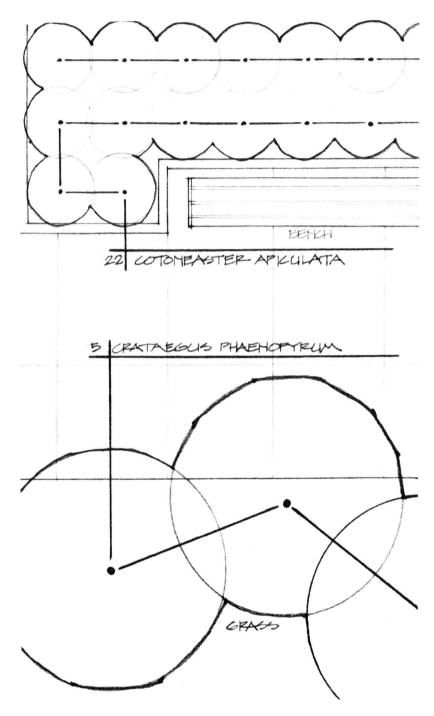

22 COTONEASTER APICULATA

5 CRATAEGUS PHAENOPYRUM

GRASS

Utility Plan

The utility plan identifies the various utility lines that exist on the site as well as those that are proposed. They include water, sewer, gas and electric. Supplemental information, such as catch basins, manholes, valves, and junction boxes, is also included.

In most instances this information is supplied by other professionals working on the design construction. However, it is important to the overall success of the design and should therefore be a primary consideration in the entire construction package.

Other Plans

Other plans often included in a construction package are location plans, which explain the general location of the project regionally, site preparation plan, demolition plan, sprinkling plan, and lighting plan.

Often plans can be combined to describe different aspects of the design construction collectively. Combinations of plans should, however, be relative to the sequence of the construction that the contractor would follow. For example, dimensioning and layout would be a more sensible combination of plans than would dimensioning and planting plans.

SCERA COMMUNITY PARK
OREM, UTAH

Woodruff Jensen _____ Date Feb 7, 1978
Woodruff Jensen, Chairman of the Board of Directors

M. Dover Hunt _____ Date Feb 7-1978
M. Dover Hunt, Manager

Maas & Grassli
Planners · Landscape Architects
Ogden, Utah

Markham & Markham
Architects · Engineers
Provo, Utah

Adamson Engineering
Structural Engineers
Ogden, Utah

Nielson Engineering
Electrical Engineers
Salt Lake City, Utah

Layout   L1-L6
Restroom Addition   A1-A2
Planting and Lighting   P1-P7
Irrigation   I1-I5
Details   D1-D6
Phasing Plan

162

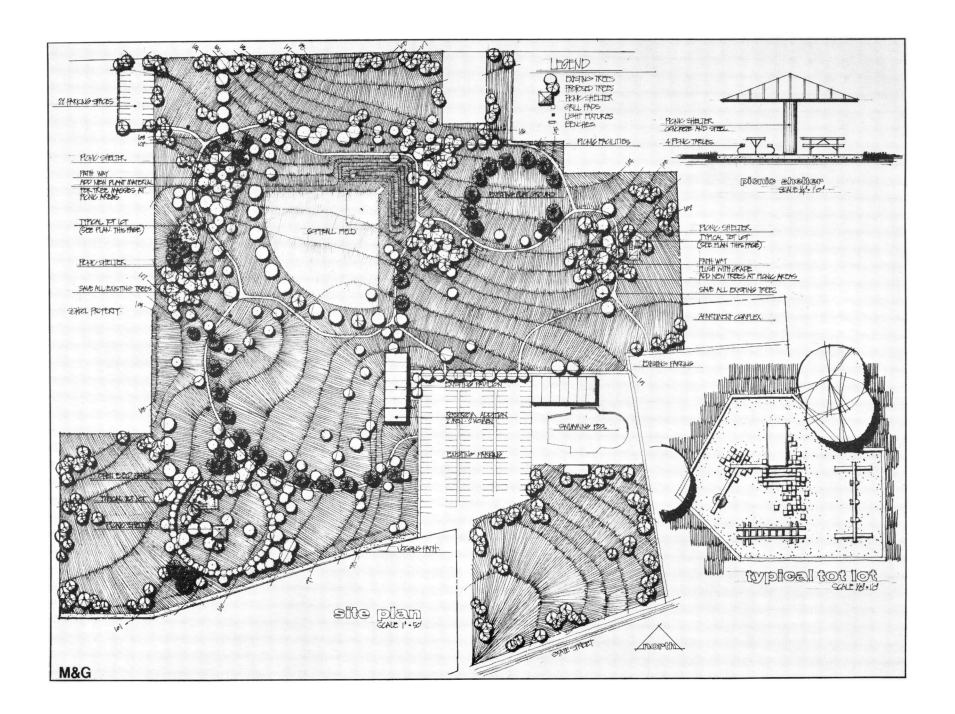

LEGEND
EXISTING TREES
PROPOSED TREES
PICNIC SHELTER
GRILL PADS
LIGHT FIXTURES
BENCHES

PICNIC FACILITIES

PICNIC SHELTER
CONCRETE AND STEEL
4 PICNIC TABLES

picnic shelter
SCALE ⅛" = 1'-0"

22 PARKING SPACES

PICNIC SHELTER

PATH WAY
ADD NEW PLANT MATERIAL
FOR TREE MASSES AT
PICNIC AREAS

TYPICAL TOT LOT
(SEE PLAN THIS PAGE)

PICNIC SHELTER

SAVE ALL EXISTING TREES

SCHOOL PROPERTY

SOFTBALL FIELD

EXISTING PLAYGROUND

PICNIC SHELTER

TYPICAL TOT LOT
(SEE PLAN THIS PAGE)

PATH WAY
FLUSH WITH GRADE
ADD NEW TREES AT PICNIC AREAS

SAVE ALL EXISTING TREES

APARTMENT COMPLEX

EXISTING PARKING

EXISTING PAVILION

RESTROOM ADDITION
2 MEN 2 WOMEN

EXISTING PARKING

SWIMMING POOL

JOGGING PATH

TYPICAL TOT LOT

PICNIC SHELTER

site plan
SCALE 1" = 50'

STATE STREET

north

typical tot lot
SCALE ⅛" = 1'-0"

M&G

163

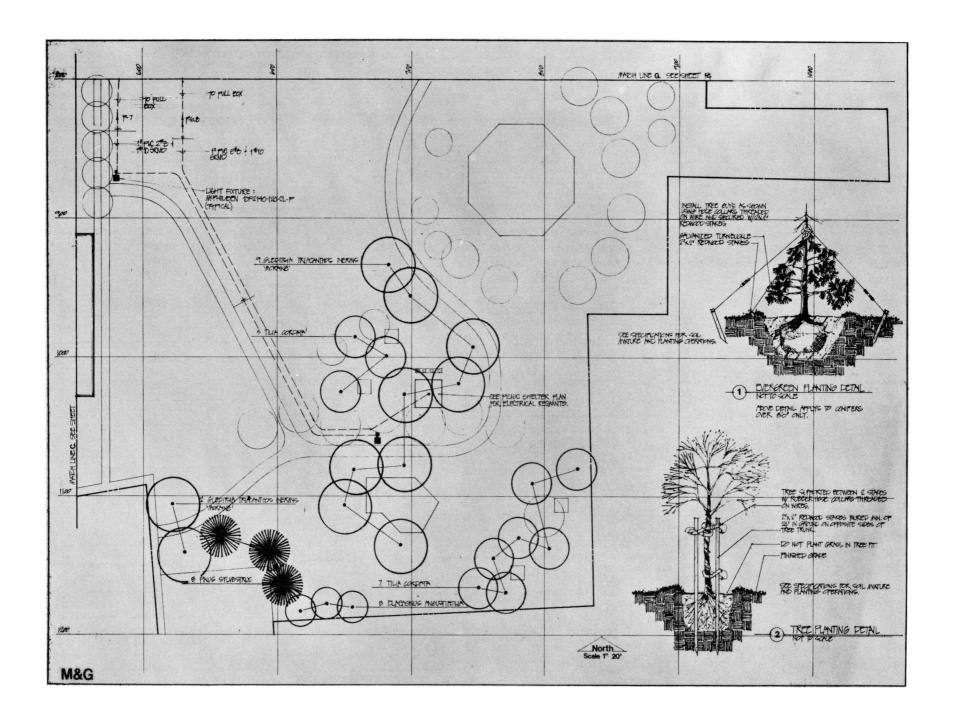

MATCH LINE G SEE SHEET 14

TO PULL BOX

TO PULL BOX

F-7

F-6.8

1" PVC 2#8 #10 GRND

1" PVC 8#8 #10 GRND

LIGHT FIXTURE:
MCPHILBEN 10F2140-120-CL-P
(TYPICAL)

9 GLEDITSIA TRIACANTHOS INERMIS
'MORAINE'

5 TILIA CORDATA

SEE PICNIC SHELTER PLAN
FOR ELECTRICAL REQMNTS.

2 GLEDITSIA TRIACANTHOS INERMIS
'MORAINE'

8 PINUS SYLVESTRIS

7 TILIA CORDATA

8 ELAEAGNUS ANGUSTIFOLIA

MATCH LINE C. SEE SHEET

North
Scale 1" 20'

INSTALL TREE GUYS AS SHOWN
USING HOSE COLLARS THREADED
ON WIRE AND SECURED W/ 2"x2"
REDWOOD STAKES

GALVANIZED TURNBUCKLE
2"x2" REDWOOD STAKES

SEE SPECIFICATIONS FOR SOIL
MIXTURE AND PLANTING OPERATIONS.

① EVERGREEN PLANTING DETAIL
NOT TO SCALE

ABOVE DETAIL APPLIES TO CONIFERS
OVER 60" ONLY.

TREE SUPPORTED BETWEEN 2 STAKES
W/ RUBBER HOSE COLLARS THREADED
ON WIRES

2"x2" REDWOOD STAKES BURIED MIN. OF
24" IN GROUND ON OPPOSITE SIDES OF
TREE TRUNK.

DO NOT PLANT GRASS IN TREE PIT.

FINISHED GRADE

SEE SPECIFICATIONS FOR SOIL MIXTURE
AND PLANTING OPERATIONS.

② TREE PLANTING DETAIL
NOT TO SCALE

M&G

164

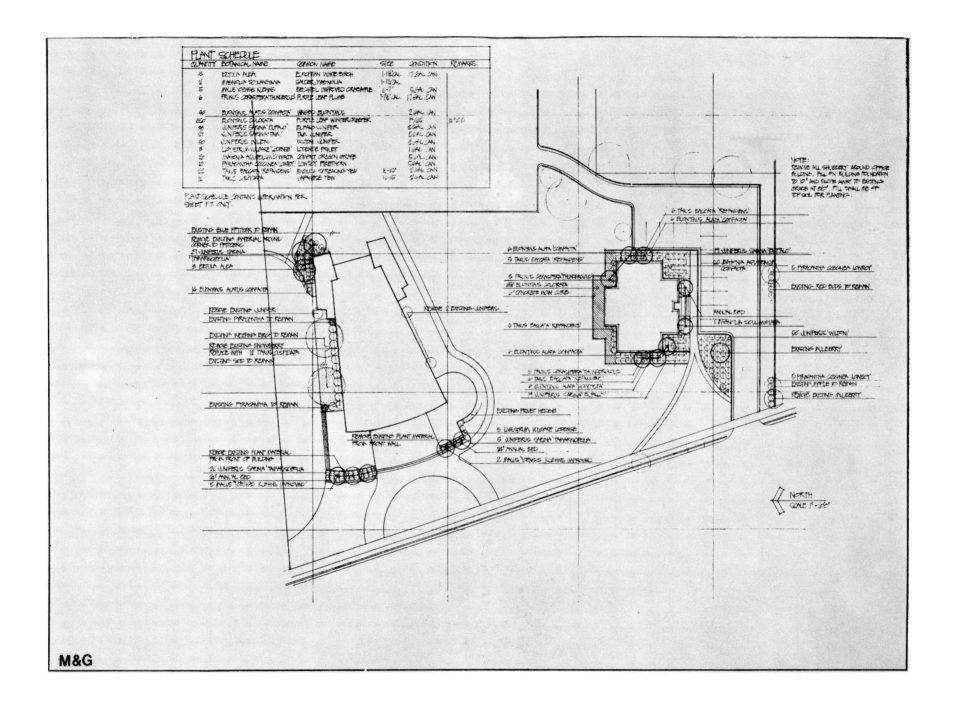

M&G

165

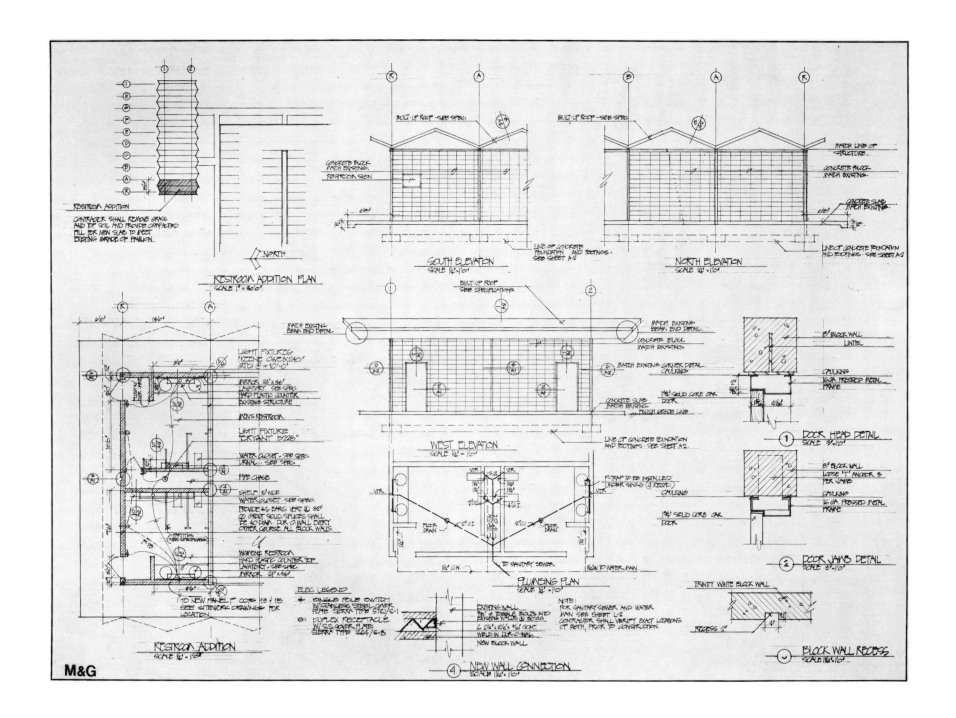

RESTROOM ADDITION

CONTRACTOR SHALL REMOVE GRASS AND TOP SOIL AND PROVIDE COMPACTED FILL PER NEW SLAB TO MEET EXISTING GRADE OF PAVILION.

NORTH

RESTROOM ADDITION PLAN
SCALE 1" = 30'-0"

SOUTH ELEVATION
SCALE 1/4"=1'-0"

NORTH ELEVATION
SCALE 1/4"=1'-0"

WEST ELEVATION
SCALE 1/4" = 1'-0"

PLUMBING PLAN
SCALE 1/4"=1'-0"

RESTROOM ADDITION
SCALE 1/4" = 1'-0"

DOOR HEAD DETAIL
SCALE 3"=1'-0"

DOOR JAMB DETAIL
SCALE 3"=1'-0"

BLOCK WALL RECESS
SCALE 1 1/2" = 1'-0"

NEW WALL CONNECTION
SCALE 1 1/2" = 1'-0"

M&G

166

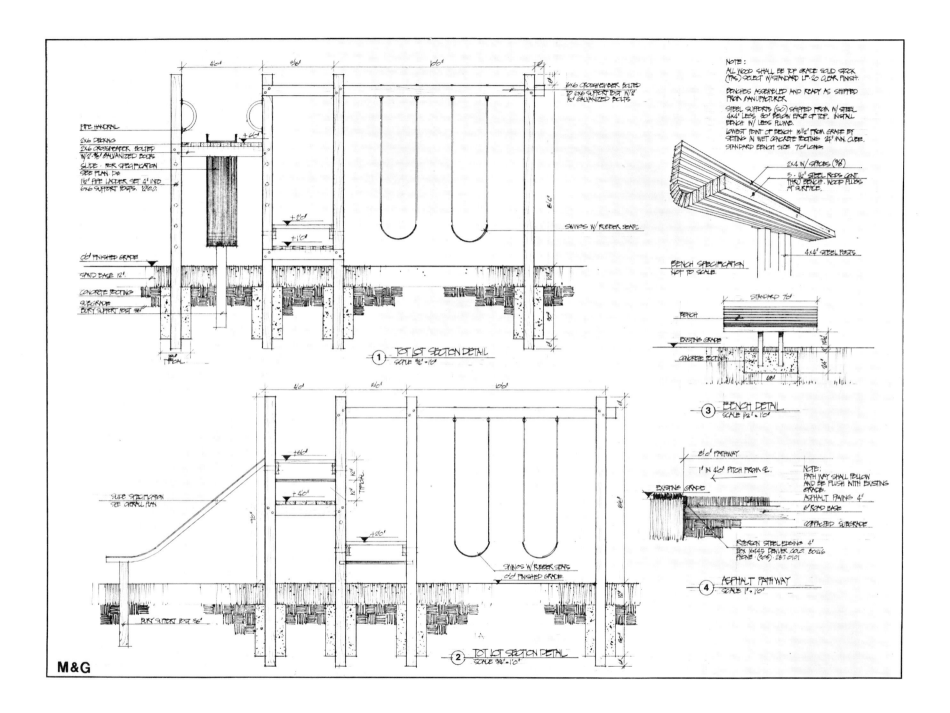

NOTE:
ALL WOOD SHALL BE R'P GRADE SOLID STOCK (PRS) SELECT W/STANDARD LP-20 CLEAR FINISH.

BENCHES ASSEMBLED AND READY AS SHIPPED FROM MANUFACTURER.

STEEL SUPPORTS (SO) SHIPPED FROM W/ STEEL 4x4' LEGS 30' BELOW EDGE OF TOP. INSTALL BENCH W/ LEGS PLUMB.
LOWEST POINT OF BENCH 16½' FROM GRADE BY SETTING IN WET CONCRETE FOOTING 24' MIN. CURE.
STANDARD BENCH SIZE 7'0' LONG.

2x4 W/ SPACES (⅜')
5 - ½" STEEL RODS CONT. THRU BENCH. WOOD PLUGS AT SURFACE.

4x4' STEEL POSTS

BENCH SPECIFICATION
NOT TO SCALE.

6x6 CROSSMEMBER BOLTED TO 6x6 SUPPORT POST W/2 ½' GALVANIZED BOLTS

PIPE HANDRAIL
2x6 DECKING
2x6 CROSSMEMBER BOLTED W/2-⅜' GALVANIZED BOLTS
SLIDE - PER SPECIFICATION SEE PLAN - D6
1½' PIPE LADDER SET 4' INTO 6x6 SUPPORT POSTS. 12'O.O.

SWINGS W/ RUBBER SEATS

0'0 FINISHED GRADE
SAND BASE 12'
CONCRETE FOOTING
SUBGRADE
BURY SUPPORT POST 36'

① TOT LOT SECTION DETAIL
SCALE ¾'-1'0'

STANDARD 7'0'
BENCH
EXISTING GRADE
CONCRETE FOOTING

③ BENCH DETAIL
SCALE ½'-1'0'

SLIDE SPECIFICATION SEE OVERALL PLAN

SWINGS W/ RUBBER SEATS
0'0 FINISHED GRADE

BURY SUPPORT POST 36'

② TOT LOT SECTION DETAIL
SCALE ⅜'-1'0'

2'0' PATHWAY
1' IN 4'0' PITCH FROM ₵.

NOTE:
PATH WAY SHALL FOLLOW AND BE FLUSH WITH EXISTING GRADE.
ASPHALT PAVING 4'
6' ROAD BASE
COMPACTED SUBGRADE

EXISTING GRADE

RYERSON STEEL EDGING 4'
BOX 16145 DENVER COLO. 80216
PHONE (303) 287-0101

④ ASPHALT PATH WAY
SCALE 1'-1'0'

M&G

167

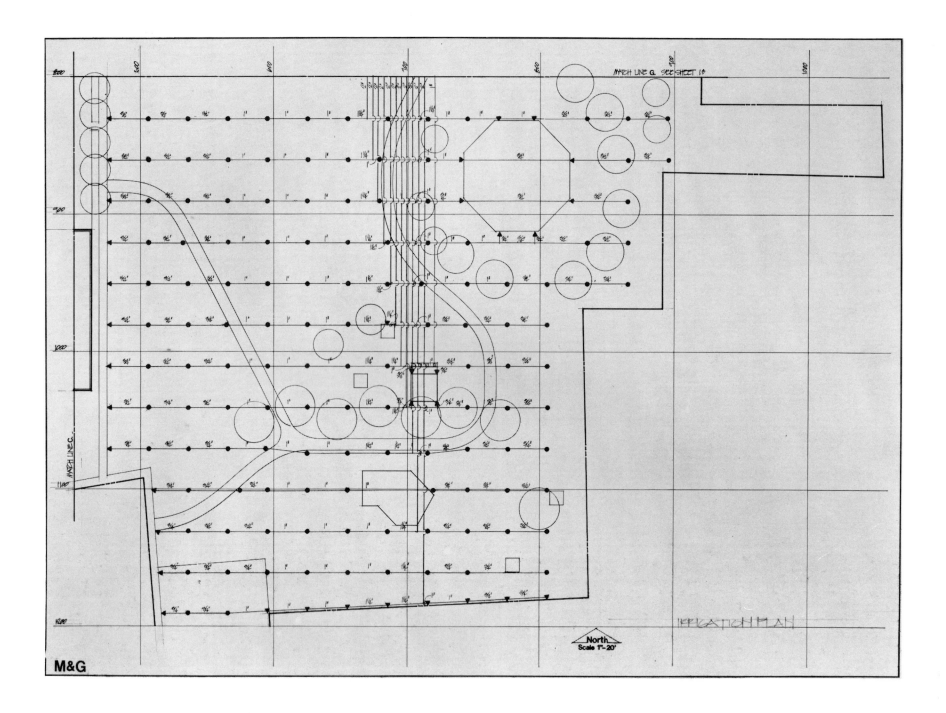

North
Scale 1"-20'

M&G

168

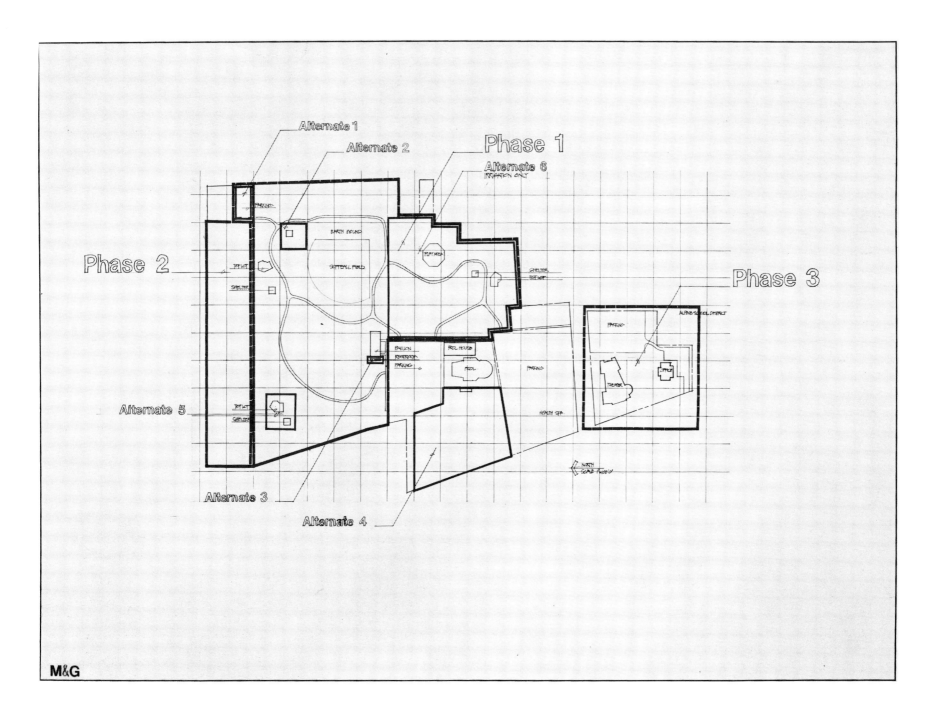

Alternate 1

Alternate 2

Phase 1

Alternate 6
IRRIGATION ONLY

EARTH MOUND

Phase 2

TOILET

SOFTBALL FIELD

SHELTER

PLAY AREA

SHELTER
REST ROOMS

Phase 3

ALPINE SCHOOL DISTRICT

PARKING

PAVILION
RESTROOM
PARKING

POOL HOUSE

POOL

PARKING

THEATER

OFFICE

Alternate 5

TOILET

SHELTER

HEALTH SPA

NORTH
SCALE 1"=100'

Alternate 3

Alternate 4

M&G

169

CONSTRUCTION AND PLANTING DETAILS

Construction details describe the specific information that relates to the structural development of the design. For each detail the designer must decide which graphic image will communicate the idea most effectively. For the most part, orthographic projections are most commonly used in detail drawings. More elaborate images such as paralines and perspectives, are often time consuming and should be used only when they represent the most practical approach.

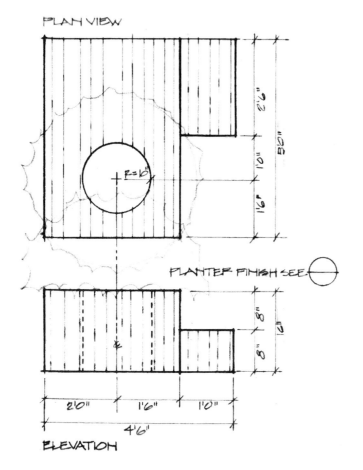

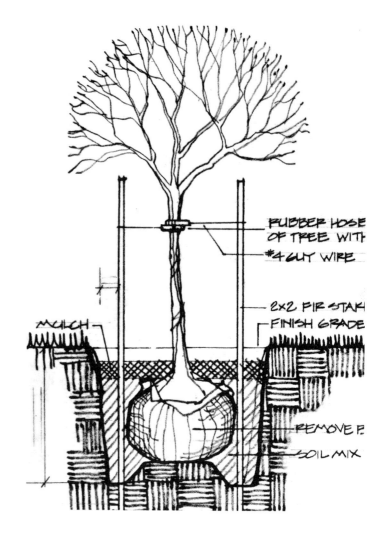

Each detail should contain information about the location of the cross reference on the parent drawing, all dimensions, building material and how they are used, and the scale and image used. Line weight variation, lettering, and look of this detail information is very important. Preplanning detail drawings on trace, will also help you organize the information before committing it to the final drawing sheet and enable you to save time erasing unexpected problems.

Details related to the planting plan are very similar to construction details, and should include the same basic information. Soil preparation, staking, and fertilizing are aspects of the planting detail that should be included.

170

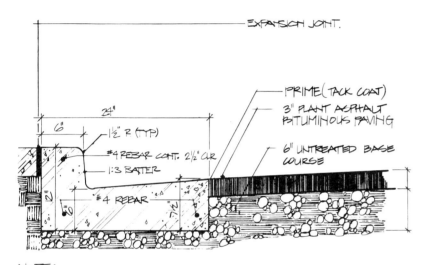

EXPANSION JOINT.

PRIME (TACK COAT)

3" PLANT ASPHALT BITUMINOUS PAVING

6" UNTREATED BASE COURSE

24"

6"

1½" R (TYP)

#4 REBAR CONT. 2½" CLR

1:3 BATER

#4 REBAR

12"

7½"

NOTE:
• WHERE SIDEWALK S ADJACENT TO CURB & GUTTER FURNISH FELT EXP. JOINT, OTHERWISE FINAL GRADE TO BE 1½" BELOW TOP OF CURB.
• LOCATE ROAD CROWN 1½" BELOW TOP OF CURB.

⊙ **Curb and Gutter / Asphalt Paving**
SCALE: 1½" = 1'-0"

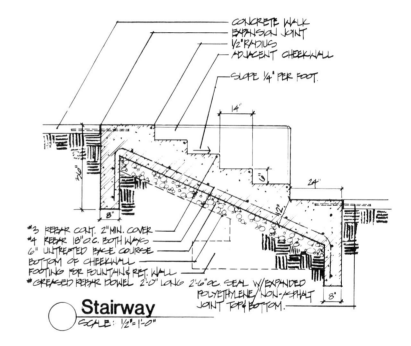

CONCRETE WALK
EXPANSION JOINT
½" RADIUS
ADJACENT CHEEKWALL

SLOPE ¼" PER FOOT

14"

8"

24"

8"

#3 REBAR CONT. 2" MIN. COVER
#4 REBAR 18" O.C. BOTH WAYS
6" UNTREATED BASE COURSE
BOTTOM OF CHEEKWALL
FOOTING FOR FOUNTAIN & RET. WALL
#4 GREASED REBAR DOWEL 2'-0" LONG 2'-6" O.C. SEAL W/EXPANDED POLYETHYLENE/NON-ASPHALT JOINT TOP & BOTTOM.

⊙ **Stairway**
SCALE: ½" = 1'-0"

171

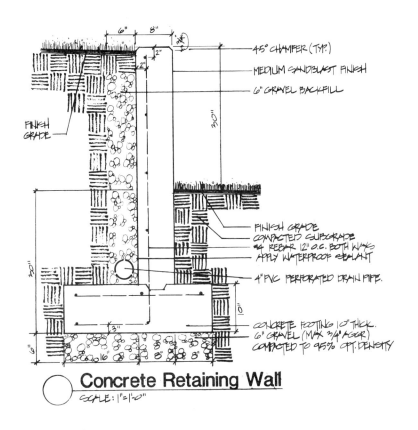

6"   8"

45° CHAMFER (TYP.)

MEDIUM SANDBLAST FINISH

6" GRAVEL BACKFILL

3'-0"

FINISH
GRADE

FINISH GRADE
COMPACTED SUBGRADE
#4 REBAR 12" O.C. BOTH WAYS
APPLY WATERPROOF SEALANT

4" PVC PERFORATED DRAIN PIPE.

30"

10"

3"

6"

CONCRETE FOOTING 10" THICK.
6" GRAVEL (MAX 3/4" AGGR)
COMPACTED TO 95% OPT. DENSITY

16"   8"   8"

Concrete Retaining Wall
SCALE: 1"=1'-0"

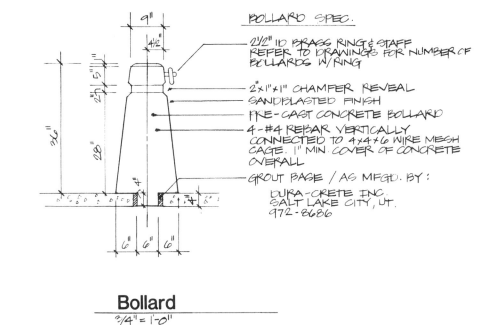

9"

4½"

BOLLARD SPEC.

2½" ID BRASS RING & STAFF
REFER TO DRAWINGS FOR NUMBER OF
BOLLARDS W/ RING

2"x1"x1" CHAMFER REVEAL
SANDBLASTED FINISH

PRE-CAST CONCRETE BOLLARD

4-#4 REBAR VERTICALLY
CONNECTED TO 4x4x6 WIRE MESH
CAGE. 1" MIN. COVER OF CONCRETE
OVERALL

GROUT BASE / AS MFGD. BY:

DURA-CRETE INC.
SALT LAKE CITY, UT.
972-8686

36"

28"

5"

2"

4"

6"   6"   6"

Bollard
3/4" = 1'-0"

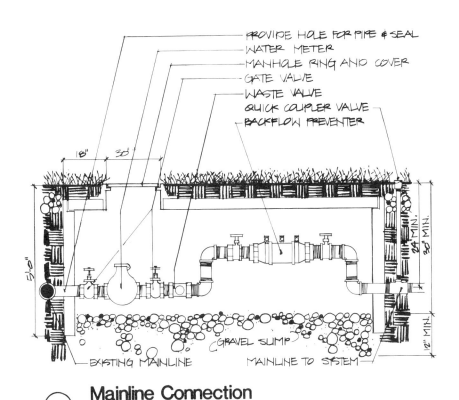

- PROVIDE HOLE FOR PIPE & SEAL
- WATER METER
- MANHOLE RING AND COVER
- GATE VALVE
- WASTE VALVE
- QUICK COUPLER VALVE
- BACKFLOW PREVENTER

18"
30"
24" MIN.
30" MIN.
5'-0"
12" MIN.

EXISTING MAINLINE
GRAVEL SUMP
MAINLINE TO SYSTEM

Mainline Connection
NOT TO SCALE

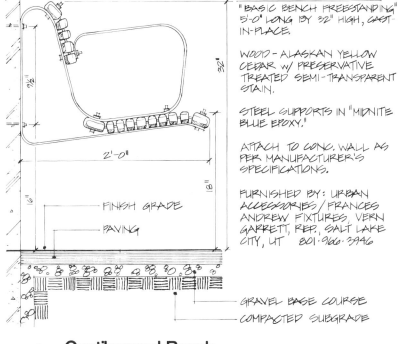

BENCH SPEC.
"BASIC BENCH FREESTANDING"
5'-0" LONG BY 32" HIGH, CAST-IN-PLACE.

WOOD - ALASKAN YELLOW CEDAR w/ PRESERVATIVE TREATED SEMI-TRANSPARENT STAIN.

STEEL SUPPORTS IN "MIDNITE BLUE EPOXY."

ATTACH TO CONC. WALL AS PER MANUFACTURER'S SPECIFICATIONS.

FURNISHED BY: URBAN ACCESSORIES / FRANCES ANDREW FIXTURES, VERN GARRETT, REP., SALT LAKE CITY, UT 801·966·3946

9½"
32"
2'-0"
18"
16"

FINISH GRADE
PAVING

GRAVEL BASE COURSE
COMPACTED SUBGRADE

Cantilevered Bench
NOT TO SCALE

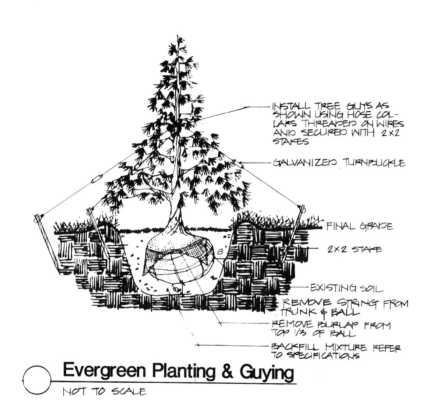

INSTALL TREE GUYS AS SHOWN USING HOSE COL-LARS THREADED ON WIRES AND SECURED WITH 2×2 STAKES

GALVANIZED TURNBUCKLE

FINAL GRADE

2×2 STAKE

EXISTING SOIL

REMOVE STRING FROM TRUNK & BALL

REMOVE BURLAP FROM TOP 1/3 OF BALL

BACKFILL MIXTURE REFER TO SPECIFICATIONS

8"

Evergreen Planting & Guying
NOT TO SCALE

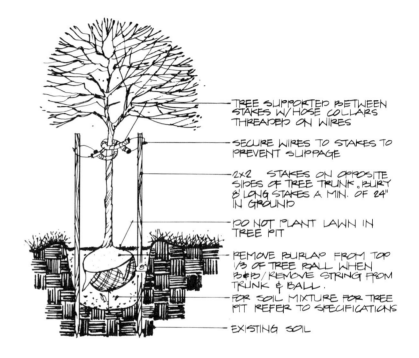

TREE SUPPORTED BETWEEN STAKES W/ HOSE COLLARS THREADED ON WIRES

SECURE WIRES TO STAKES TO PREVENT SLIPPAGE

2×2 STAKES ON OPPOSITE SIDES OF TREE TRUNK. BURY 8' LONG STAKES A MIN. OF 24" IN GROUND

DO NOT PLANT LAWN IN TREE PIT

REMOVE BURLAP FROM TOP 1/3 OF TREE BALL WHEN B & B / REMOVE STRING FROM TRUNK & BALL.

FOR SOIL MIXTURE FOR TREE PIT REFER TO SPECIFICATIONS

EXISTING SOIL

8"

Deciduous Planting & Staking
NOT TO SCALE

Schedules and Profiles

Planting details often include a schedule or outline of the various plant materials and related information that would be too confusing or cumbersome to describe as part of the plan. These schedules usually contain the botanical and common names, number and sizes of the plants, information about delivery to the site (balled and burlapped, canned, or container grown, bare root) and any additional notes specifying the planting or maintenance. Construction details may also include schedules related to retaining wall construction or other materials that can be communicated collectively in a table or diagram.

Profiles are graphic representations of vertical alignments to a horizontal distance. They are used in calculating circulation routes and gravity flow utility lines.

Information described in profiles is presented similarly to an exaggerated section, where the vertical scale is greater than the horizontal in order to communicate the data more clearly.

RENDERING

Technical communication of construction drawings does not necessitate illustrative rendering. The key to a successful construction package is simplicity. Effective line work, lettering, and organization of the information is far more important than values, textures, and other visual communication techniques that might confuse the contractor. Illustrative rendering of construction drawings can also be very timely, and perhaps a waste of valuable resources.

Rendering with value and texture should be applied to construction drawings only in so much as it helps describe the materials or the structural relationships of the materials. The graphic images of various materials commonly used in construction have been somewhat standardized, and you should become familiar with these graphic patterns.

Values are also used as a means of describing particular elements or materials in the design construction. Water features, grasses, and other expanses of similar materials, are often depicted by a value to help distinguish them from other design elements. Values of shade and shadow are not commonly used because they are usually insignificant to the construction phase.

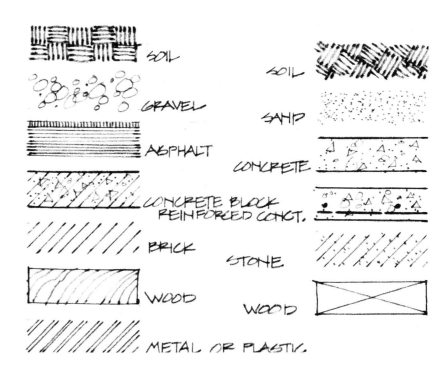

Support images, such as cars and people, are also unimportant at this phase of the design process. Images, such as trees and shrubs, however, are integral parts of the construction and various images are often utilized to define the variations in plant material. Nevertheless, the key to portraying these images, like all aspects of technical communication, is simplicity and clarity.

a. Produce a construction drawing package for the information given on the roughly drawn plan which follows. Apply the appropriate line work and lettering. Package should include:

cover sheet, layout plan, grading plan, dimensioning plan, planting plan, and detail page. Format, scale, and titleblock as individually desired. The purpose of this exercise is to expose you to the fundamentals of a construction package. The emphasis is not in the accuracy or quality of the design, but on the line lettering and look of the overall package).

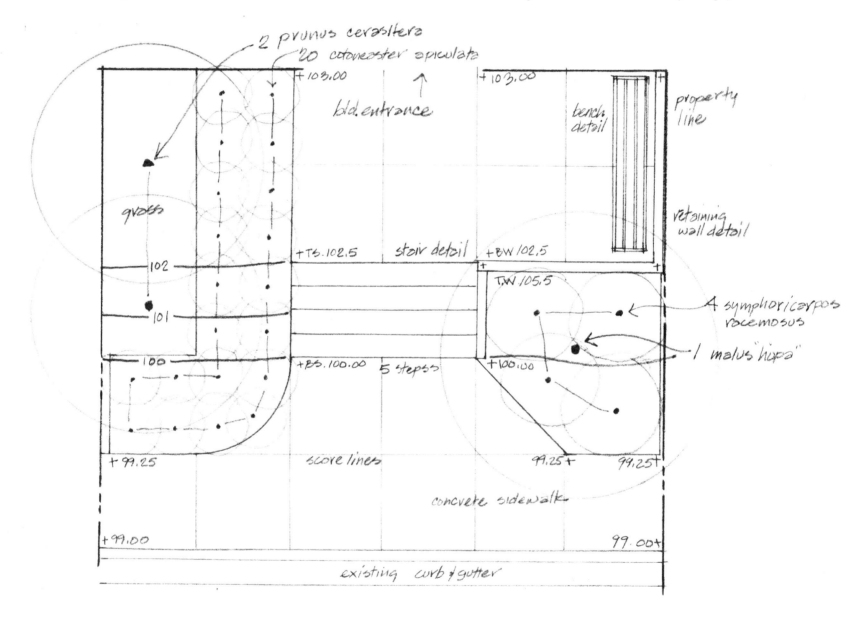

Exercise 20: FINAL EXAMINATION

a. Upon completion of this book, you should have begun to develop your own design-graphics relationships and ideas. Therefore, you should begin to develop your own approaches to design-graphics and design-graphics instruction. As a final examination you are to create your own version of this book, complete with your own ideas, and your own graphics.

REFERENCES

The following is a list of recommended books that support the information presented in the previous section.

Austin, R.L., 1984. *Site Graphics.* New York: Van Nostrand Reinhold. 128 pages.

Ching, F., 1984. *Building Construction Illustrated.* New York: Van Nostrand Reinhold. 320 pages.

de Chiara, J., Callender, J.J., 1980. *Time Saver Standards for Building Types.* New York: McGraw-Hill. 1088 pages.

de Chiara, J., Koppelman, L., 1977. *Site Planning Standards.* New York: McGraw-Hill.

Robinette, G.O., 1968. *Off the Board – Into the Ground.* Dubuque, Iowa: Wm. C. Brown Co. 367 pages.

Walker, T.D., 1985. *Site Design and Construction Detailing.* 2nd Edition. Mesa, AZ: PDA Publishers.

SECTION D

COMPUTER AIDED DRAFTING/DESIGN

10

Communication and Computers

The advent of the computer has changed the way in which many people think, work and communicate ideas--designers not to be excluded. Computer aided design and drafting equipment has revolutionized the production output of many offices. From small personal computers to large main frame computers, the ability to communicate design ideas has exploded into the world of technology. Technology, incidentally, that continues to improve so rapidly that the designer's ability to keep pace is the only limiting factor.

Computer Aided Drafting/Design, or CAD, as it is frequently referred to, is a tool that has renovated the concept of graphic communications and reconfigured the conventional approach to developing, evaluating, and refining design ideas. This chapter will suggest several advantages of computer aided graphic communication, and demonstrate a number of CAD generated examples. It must be pointed out, however, that this is only the tip of the 'computerized' iceberg and much more information is available and should be obtained.

Hardware and software packages are becoming more sophisticated in their graphic capabilities and more understandable in their application to design and graphic communication. No longer do individuals have to be computer 'whiz kids' to operate and produce design ideas rapidly and efficiently.

In past years, computers have appeared to some designers as the ominous creature from the dark side. Lack of computer experience, expense, stubbornness and general fear, have created great misunderstandings about this incredibly useful tool. The truth of the matter is, that computers provide new flexibility in design development and graphic communication. They allow the designer to concentrate efforts in producing a functional and aesthetically pleasing product.

Time consuming preparation of base information, for example, is quickly and easily produced by the computer for numerous alternative ideas and concept drawings. In many instances, designers can interface their equipment with other professionals and exchange information. This is extremely helpful on large scale projects where the exchange of accurate data is crucial.

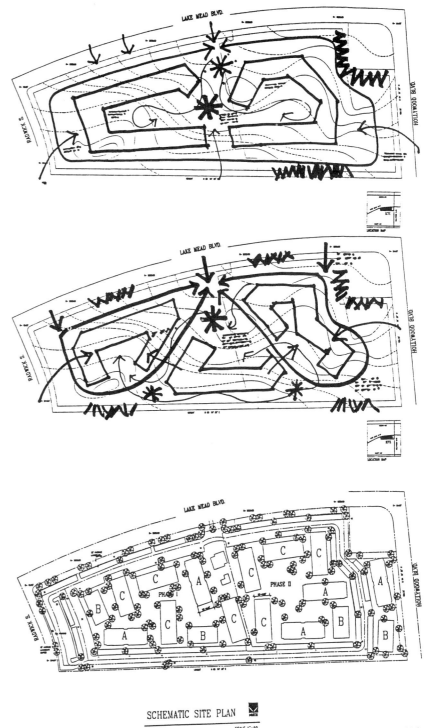

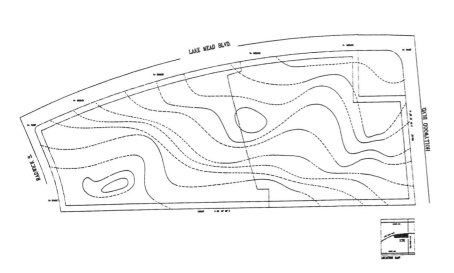

SCHEMATIC SITE PLAN

SCALE 1"=50

181

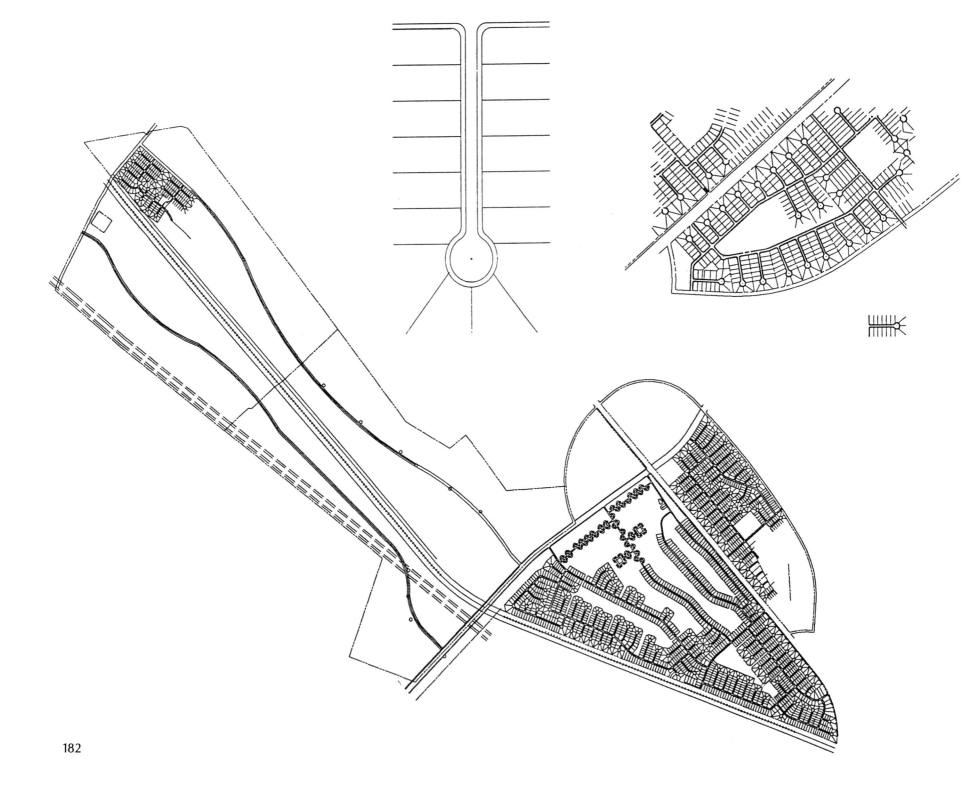

182

Also available to the designer are a variety of pre-designed elements and symbols that are congruent with the particular program in which one is working. For example, an architectural program would include such elements as doors, windows, vanities, toilets, furniture and other pre-drawn items that are easily inserted into the drawing at the appropriate location and scale. Other elements include, cross section reference, and materials symbols, arrows, benchmarks, and a number of other drawing aids.

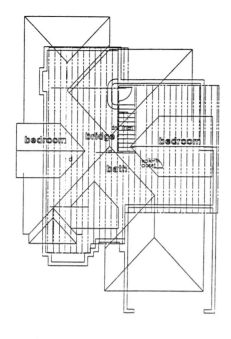

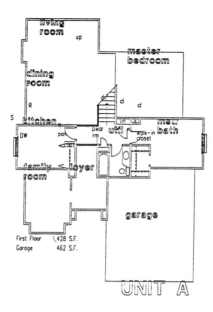

First Floor   1,428 S.F.
Garage   462 S.F.

UNIT A

Alternate Bath Plan

The CAD is typically equipped with a layering system which allows the operator to set up a series of layers of information, similar to the old 'overlay system.' Each layer, of which there may be numerous, contains specific data, existing elements, notes, buildings, walls, windows, doors, furnishings, etc.

With a simple command any layer can be removed or displayed in any combination with other layers, making the overlay process even more flexible and efficient.

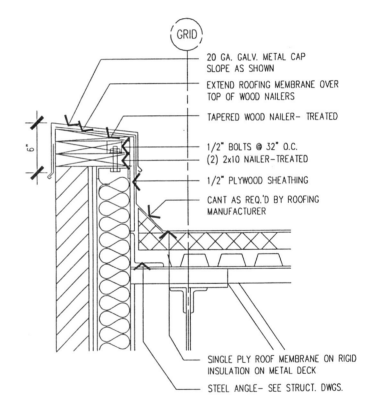

GRID

20 GA. GALV. METAL CAP SLOPE AS SHOWN

EXTEND ROOFING MEMBRANE OVER TOP OF WOOD NAILERS

TAPERED WOOD NAILER- TREATED

1/2" BOLTS @ 32" O.C.
(2) 2x10 NAILER-TREATED

1/2" PLYWOOD SHEATHING

CANT AS REQ'D BY ROOFING MANUFACTURER

SINGLE PLY ROOF MEMBRANE ON RIGID INSULATION ON METAL DECK

STEEL ANGLE- SEE STRUCT. DWGS.

6"

parapet detail
SCALE 1 1/2"= 1'-0"

D-PARA1

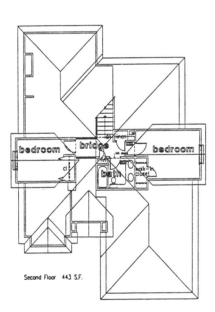

Second Floor 443 S.F.

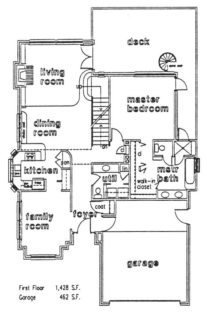

First Floor   1,428 S.F.
Garage   462 S.F.

UNIT A

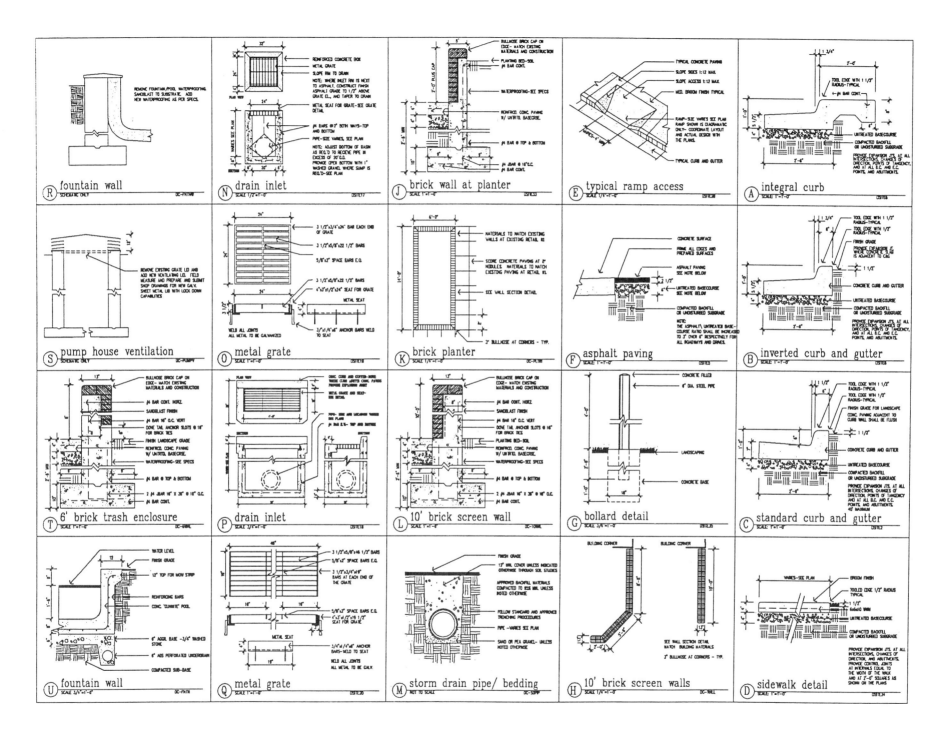

R — fountain wall — SCHEMATIC ONLY — DC-FNTNW

N — drain inlet — SCALE 1/2"=1'-0" — DSTTE17

J — brick wall at planter — SCALE 1"=1'-0" — DSTTE23

E — typical ramp access — SCALE 1/4"=1'-0" — DSTTE28

A — integral curb — DSTTE8

S — pump house ventilation — SCHEMATIC ONLY — DC-PUMPV

O — metal grate — SCALE 1"=1'-0" — DSTTE19

K — brick planter — SCALE 1/4"=1'-0" — DC-PLTR

F — asphalt paving — DSTTE9

B — inverted curb and gutter — SCALE 1"=1'-0" — DSTTE10

T — 6' brick trash enclosure — SCALE 1"=1'-0" — DC-6BRWL

P — drain inlet — SCALE 3/4"=1'-0" — DSTTE18

L — 10' brick screen wall — SCALE 1"=1'-0" — DC-TOWRL

G — bollard detail — SCALE 3/4"=1'-0" — DSTTE25

C — standard curb and gutter — SCALE 1"=1'-0" — DSTTE11

U — fountain wall — SCALE 3/4"=1'-0" — DC-FNTN

Q — metal grate — SCALE 1"=1'-0" — DSTTE20

M — storm drain pipe/ bedding — NOT TO SCALE — DC-SDPIP

H — 10' brick screen walls — SCALE 1/4"=1'-0" — DC-10BRL

D — sidewalk detail — SCALE 1"=1'-0" — DSTTE34

185

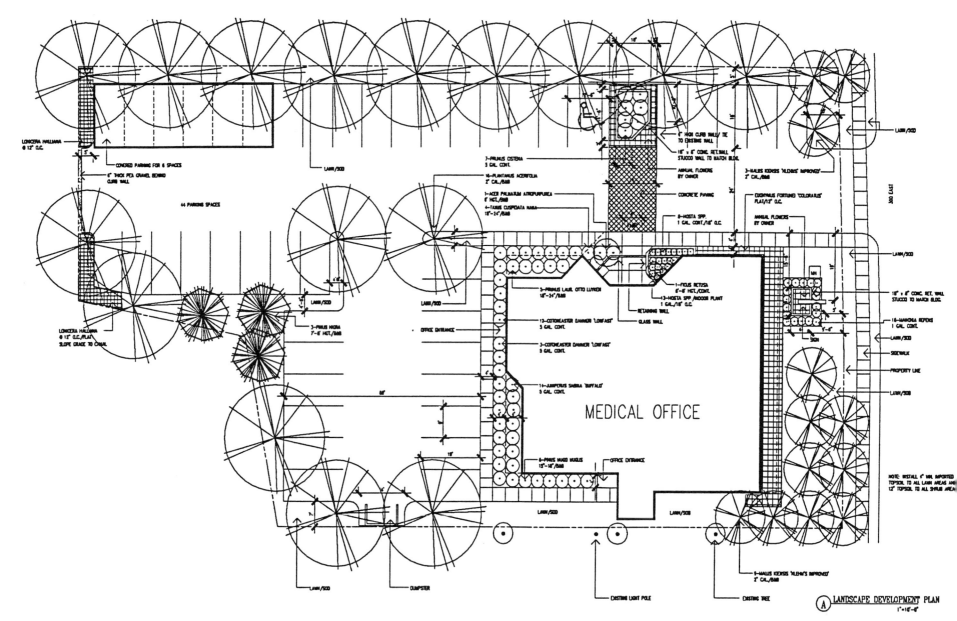

LONICERA HALLIANA
@ 12" O.C.

COVERED PARKING FOR 6 SPACES
6" THICK PEA GRAVEL BEHIND
CURB WALL

44 PARKING SPACES

LONICERA HALLIANA
@ 12" O.C./FLAT
SLOPE GRADE TO CANAL

3-PINUS NIGRA
7'-8' HGT./B&B

LAWN /SOD

OFFICE ENTRANCE

LAWN /SOD

LAWN /SOD

DUMPSTER

LAWN /SOD

7-PRUNUS CISTENA
3 GAL. CONT.

16-PLANTANUS ACERIFOLIA
2" CAL./B&B

1-ACER PALMATUM ATROPURPUREA
6' HGT./B&B

4-TAXUS CUSPIDATA NANA
18"-24"/B&B

5-PRUNUS LAUR. OTTO LUYKEN
18"-24"/B&B

13-COTONEASTER DAMMERI 'LOWFAST'
5 GAL. CONT.

3-COTONEASTER DAMMERI 'LOWFAST'
5 GAL. CONT.

10-JUNIPERUS SABINA 'BUFFALO'
5 GAL. CONT.

6-PINUS MUGO MUGUS
15"-18"/B&B

OFFICE ENTRANCE

4" HIGH CURB WALL/ TIE
TO EXISTING WALL

18" x 8" CONC. RET. WALL
STUCCO WALL TO MATCH BLDG.

ANNUAL FLOWERS
BY OWNER

CONCRETE PAVING

8-HOSTA SPP.
1 GAL. CONT./18" O.C.

1-FICUS RETUSA

43-HOSTA SPP./INDOOR PLANT
1 GAL./18" O.C.

RETAINING WALL

GLASS WALL

3-MALUS KIENSIS 'KLEHMS IMPROVED'
2" CAL./B&B

EUONYMUS FORTUNEI 'COLORATUS'
FLAT/12" O.C.

ANNUAL FLOWERS
BY OWNER

300 EAST

LAWN /SOD

LAWN /SOD

18" x 8" CONC. RET. WALL
STUCCO TO MATCH BLDG.

18-MAHONIA REPENS
1 GAL. CONT.

LAWN /SOD

SIDEWALK

PROPERTY LINE

LAWN /SOD

MH

SIGN

MEDICAL OFFICE

NOTE: INSTALL 6" MIN. IMPORTED
TOPSOIL TO ALL LAWN AREAS AND
12" TOPSOIL TO ALL SHRUB AREAS

9-MALUS KIENSIS 'KLEHM'S IMPROVED'
2" CAL./B&B

EXISTING LIGHT POLE

EXISTING TREE

Ⓐ LANDSCAPE DEVELOPMENT PLAN
1"=10'-0"

NORTH

186

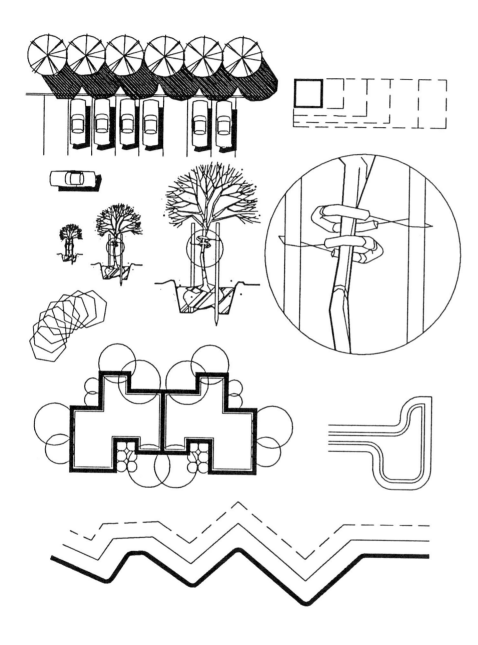

Computer aided graphic production is incredibly precise with regard to the information entered in, and yet extremely flexible in its ability to manipulate that information. For example, very accurate detailed elements of a design once entered, can very quickly be copied, moved, repeated, enlarged, reduced, or any number of options available to the designer. This also true with regard to complex pieces of information, such as large scale master plans, or intricate details. With a simple push button command, they can be rotated, mirrored, skewed, accented, or several other possible alterations.

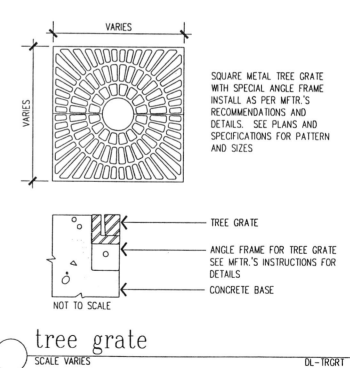

VARIES

VARIES

SQUARE METAL TREE GRATE
WITH SPECIAL ANGLE FRAME
INSTALL AS PER MFTR.'S
RECOMMENDATIONS AND
DETAILS. SEE PLANS AND
SPECIFICATIONS FOR PATTERN
AND SIZES

TREE GRATE

ANGLE FRAME FOR TREE GRATE
SEE MFTR.'S INSTRUCTIONS FOR
DETAILS

CONCRETE BASE

NOT TO SCALE

tree grate
SCALE VARIES

DL-TRGRT

187

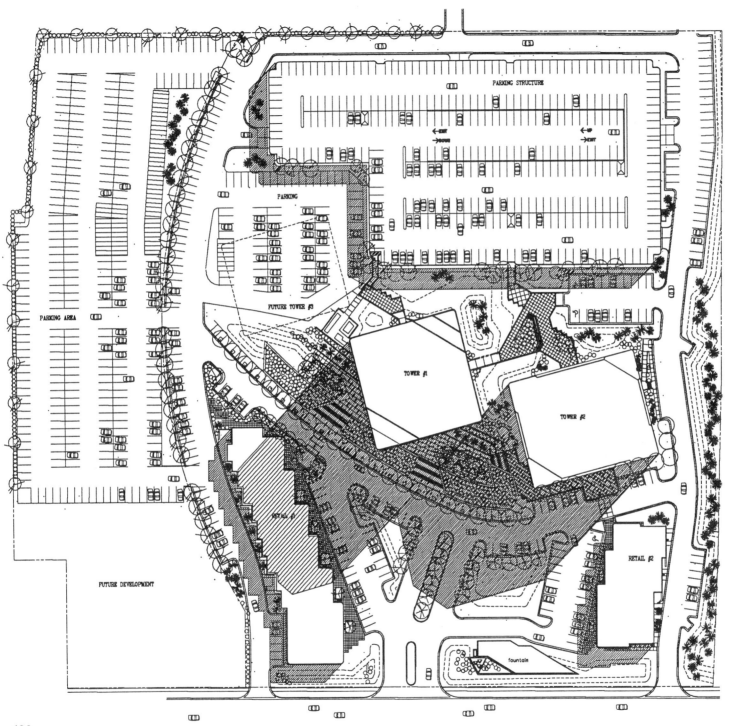

PARKING STRUCTURE

PARKING

FUTURE TOWER #3

PARKING AREA

TOWER #1

TOWER #2

RETAIL #1

RETAIL #2

FUTURE DEVELOPMENT

fountain

Woodlands
Business
Park

Master Plan '89

NORTH

SCALE 1"=30'-0"

188

State and Vine Plaza
SHOPPING CENTER

APARTMENT COMMUNITY
MACHAN HAMPSHIRE PROPERTIES, INC.

TYPE A

COUNTRY

SHEET NO.

F3

CORNERS

ENTRANCE

Loading and Service Areas

(T) **6' brick**
SCALE 1"=1'-0"

PLAZA CENTRE
EXISTING ELEMENTS

OLDTOWN

𝕽𝕺𝕬𝕯𝖂𝕬𝖄 𝕾𝕿𝕬𝕿𝕴𝕺𝕹

PLAN

Notes, legends, titles and text are easily applied to drawings in a variety of styles and fonts. No longer does the designer spend tedious hours hand lettering, applying press-on letters, mechanical lettering or using sticky backs. Depending on the complexity of the programming, CAD equipment can provide a number of pre-designated lettering types or even create new ones.

Dimensioning with the computer is quick, easy and extremely accurate. Dimension lines, extension lines, and arrows are inserted at the touch of a finger and the dimension is calculated by the computer and applied.

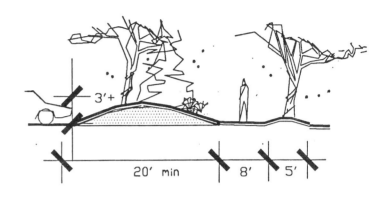

20' min   8'   5'

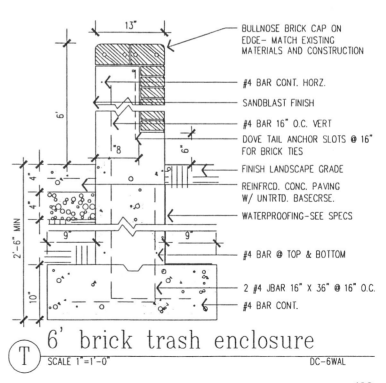

- BULLNOSE BRICK CAP ON EDGE— MATCH EXISTING MATERIALS AND CONSTRUCTION
- #4 BAR CONT. HORZ.
- SANDBLAST FINISH
- #4 BAR 16" O.C. VERT
- DOVE TAIL ANCHOR SLOTS @ 16" FOR BRICK TIES
- FINISH LANDSCAPE GRADE
- REINFRCD. CONC. PAVING W/ UNTRTD. BASECRSE.
- WATERPROOFING-SEE SPECS
- #4 BAR @ TOP & BOTTOM
- 2 #4 JBAR 16" X 36" @ 16" O.C.
- #4 BAR CONT.

(T) **6' brick trash enclosure**
SCALE 1"=1'-0"   DC-6WAL

189

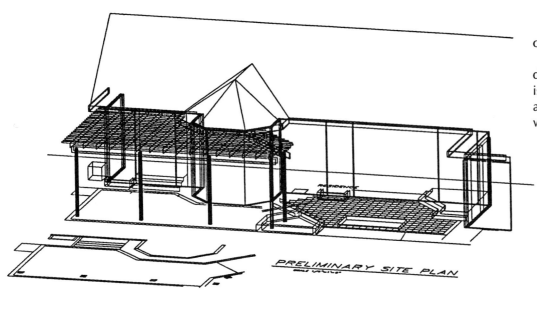

PRELIMINARY SITE PLAN

Computers have made great advancements in the realms of two and three dimensional graphic communication as well. Depending upon the complexity of the data entered, a designer can have at his disposal elevations, perspectives, isometrics, sections and other orthographics and have the ability to manipulate these images in such a way as to literally walk through a graphic environment.

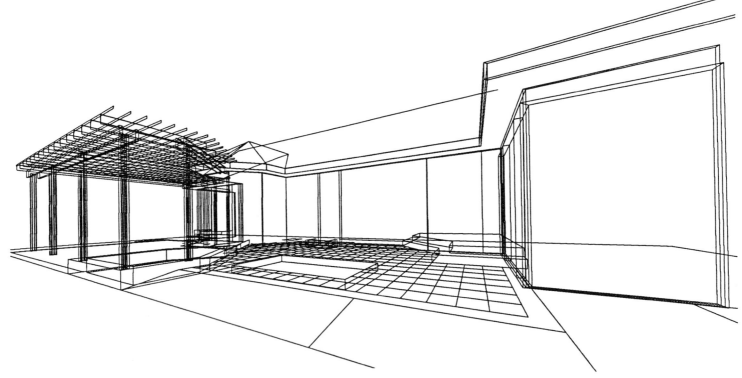

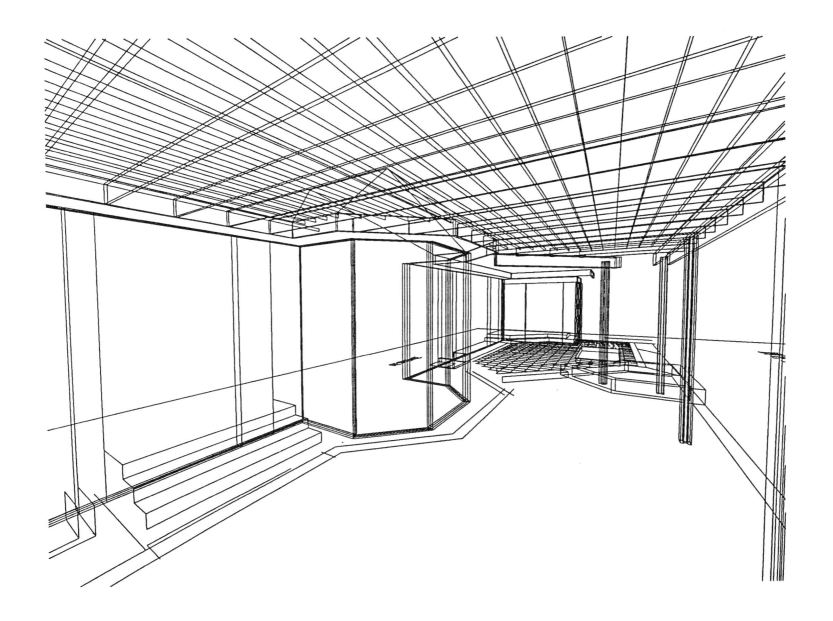

192

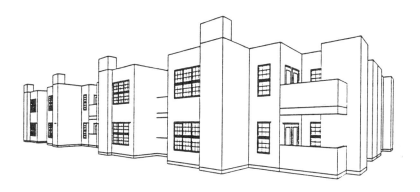

With the aid of the computer, perspective construction is easily and accurately produced in a matter of minutes. Many designers use CAD to produce the framework for a sketch and then with simple modifications can provide the final product.

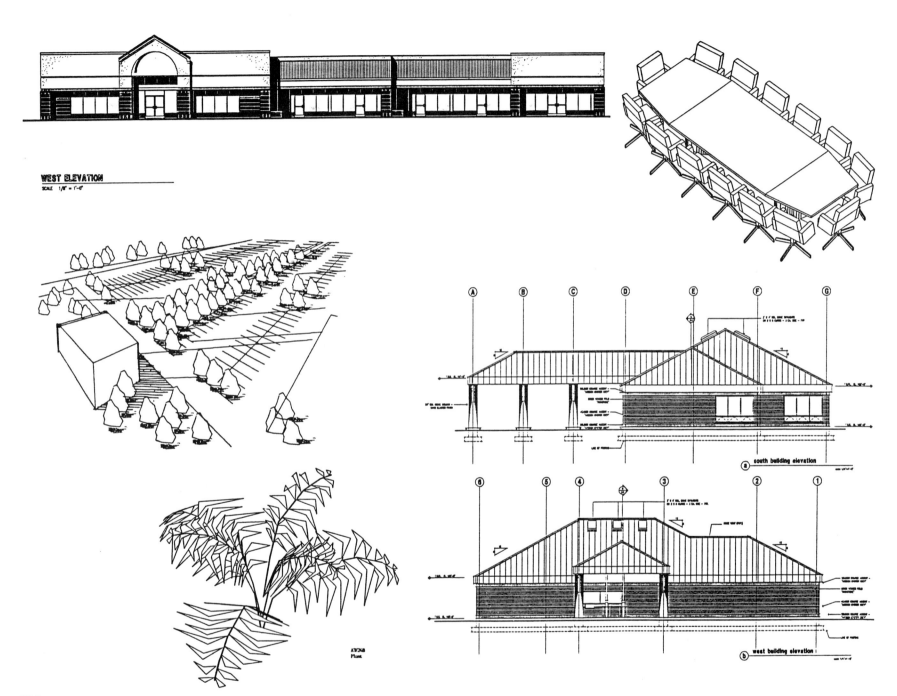

WEST ELEVATION

SCALE 1/8" = 1'-0"

south building elevation

west building elevation

194

The refinement and communications of these computerized ideas can range from something as simple as a rough line perspective sketch to a presentation piece as realistic as a photograph, complete with calibrated sun angles, reflections and shadows.

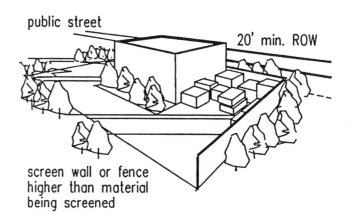

public street

20' min. ROW

screen wall or fence higher than material being screened

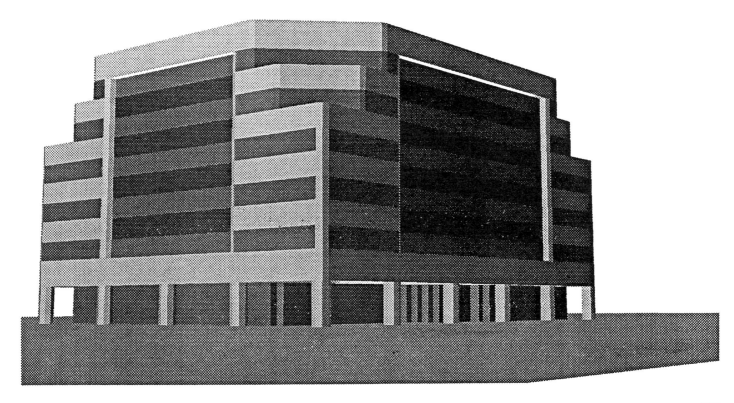

Another area greatly enhanced and increasingly demanded by the designers, is the ability to convert graphic ideas and design elements into quantitative figures and dollar amounts. Again, the computer's capacity to 'run the numbers' is only limited by the designer's ability to input the information. Area take-offs, quantities, schedules, itemizations and other calculations are all readily accessible.

As CAD equipment becomes more available and affordable, many designers are choosing to convert from the traditional pen and pencil to the technology of the disk drive and display screen. And, as in the case with most equipment, the more elaborate the machinery, the more refined the product. And typically, the more expensive the cost. Therefore, as one makes the transition from conventional to CAD, make sure that the equipment fits the need and speed of the operator.

INDEX